BUY
YOUR FIRST
HOME
TODAY!

Empower Your Life
Build Your Wealth
Own the Home of Your Dreams

JOHN W. MALLETT

PROSPERITY
MEDIA VENTURES

2019 EDITION

COPYRIGHT © 2019 BY JOHN MALLETT

ALL RIGHTS RESERVED

ISBN #978-0-9985608-0-9

No part of this publication may be reproduced, stored in a retrieval system, or transmitted in any form or by any means, electronic, mechanical, photocopying, recording, scanning, or otherwise, except as permitted by the author.

ABOUT THE AUTHOR

John W. Mallett has personally originated over one billion dollars in mortgage loans over the last two decades. Many people refer to John as *America's Homeownership Coach*™, with the unique ability to demystify the complexity of mortgages into easy to understand concepts. John is the founder and President of MainStreet Mortgage, located in Westlake Village, California. He received his undergraduate degree from Brigham Young University and an MBA degree from the University of Southern California. John and his wife, Carol, are the parents of three phenomenally talented and amazing children and reside in Southern California.

ACKNOWLEDGMENTS

Six years ago at 2am in the morning, I finished the first draft of my book. Late at night for months, I typed every word myself while sitting on the couch in my living room with my laptop. There was one problem. After reading the manuscript, I thought, "This is the most boring book I have ever read on mortgage financing." I'd fallen short of writing a book that was interesting, easy to understand, and educated people about the most important investment they will ever make.

I needed big time help. Remarkably, it came in unexpected ways at exactly the right moment. The result of all that effort on the part of many people, is the creation of what you are holding in your hands—a book on mortgage financing that I hope you will find interesting, informative, and easy to understand. As I learned over many years, that is no small task when it comes to the complexities of home financing.

I would like to thank my good friend Kevin O'Donnell who told me "I had to write a book" and helped me take the first baby steps as an author. I am deeply grateful to Ken Corr who is a friend, mentor, a writing and life coach. This book would not have materialized without Ken's support. Special thanks to Scott Coady, my life coach and friend, who has given me so many lessons and been a catalyst for life changes for which I am profoundly grateful.

I am particularly indebted to Ramona Rowen. She does not know this, but the lunch we had at Jack's discussing deeper thoughts about homeownership was a turning point. I am incredibly appreciative for the many volunteer readers who provided phenomenal support, giving generously of their time to read the manuscript and share their comments. They include Theresa Smith, Joelle Hannah, Noah Crowe, and Maria Chen – a fantastic loan officer and owner of *The Loan Story*. There is Kathy Brown, an excellent loan officer and owner with Liberty Financial, and the Parkside Lending team, including my dear friend Vince Lombardo, Greg Schatz, Brooke Roehrick, Andrea Collette, and Kevin Moreen. Special thanks to Karen Bennett for her detailed work, and to Royal Peterson, Ken Mallett and Lance Vance. Kudos to Christopher Smith for his exceptional insights and encouragement.

A special thanks to my extended family Joanie and Richard Young for their support and mentoring that provided the environment to grow and refine my skills as a mortgage professional. Gratitude to Bill Carter and Arden Hjelm for their unending support and encouragement. Above all I am in deep gratitude to my wife Carol who I love and adore and for her steadfast patience and support.

TABLE OF CONTENTS

CHAPTER 2

PART 2:

KNOWLEDGE IS POWER 47

CHAPTER 3 48

INTRODUCTION

HELPING YOU BECOME A HOMEOWNER IS PERSONAL

My father walked out on our family when I was eight years old. Whatever financial security we had was gone in a heartbeat. I was the youngest of four siblings, and from then on we were raised by my single mom. She did everything in her power to keep our family afloat, but our descent into deep poverty was relentless. Within a few years, we went from living in a nice house in a beach community to barely surviving in an apartment in a federal housing project where the career path for many of my school friends began in juvenile hall, advanced to the county jail, and ended in prison.

When I was twelve, our lives suffered another hard blow when Mom was diagnosed with multiple sclerosis. It fell to me to be her caregiver. We survived on food stamps, welfare checks, the support of our church, and various odd jobs I picked up, from delivering newspapers to selling Christmas cards door to door. Somehow we managed to keep things together.

My mother died suddenly when I was 18 years old. It hit home how fragile life is and how, in spite of hard work, a good heart, and the best of intentions, people can spend their entire lives on the edge financially, not knowing from week to week if there will be a roof over their head and food on their plate. Deep inside, I knew it didn't have to be that way, and there was something better for myself and for others. This sense of possibility propelled me forward. After supporting myself through college, I chose to enter the home financing industry. It was here that I discovered that my intuition was right and financial security and abundance are possible for almost everyone.

Jump forward to 2007 when the subprime catastrophe hit and the housing market crashed. I was on the front lines seeing it all happen before my eyes; people coming to me who had gotten risky loans from unscrupulous lenders and were losing everything—not just their homes, but their relationships and their health. I knew it didn't have to be this way, and now I understood where people had gone wrong. I had the knowledge to help people—if they would listen— and make sure this never happened to them again. I could show them a better path forward so their new home would be a source of financial security that could never be taken away.

I could no longer stand on the sidelines and felt called to write this book.

I understand that you bought this book because you're focused on the initial sprint to get the best financing you can to buy your new home. I guarantee this book will give you the insider information and tools you need to implement a strategy to secure that financing. But buying your home is just the first step on your journey. My goal is helping you see how success is ultimately measured by a combination of getting the right mortgage AND managing your mortgage, so you keep as much money in your pocket and as little as possible going into your lender's until you own your home free and clear. This combination of a strong initial sprint AND a successful long distance race is the key to turning your home into a source of financial security and a key element to achieving a balanced life.

Before getting into the specifics of a winning strategy for obtaining the ideal home loan, I want to share with you a principle that I adhere to which is that Homeownership is a Sacred Trust™. Here are the key attributes of this principle and why I believe it can serve as a valuable guide for new homeowners:

- Respecting that your new home is a sacred trust means understanding that what you are buying is not just a house— it is your and your family's home, the setting for many of your most rewarding personal and family experiences.

- Respecting that your home is a sacred trust means understanding that it's an investment unlike any other. Buying other real estate in addition to your home can be an excellent investment, and comparing those investments to investing in the market makes great sense. But the return on the investment in a home where you live, where your children grow up, and where you and your partner may grow old, involves the experiences shared there and the security it provides into retirement. That return on investment is priceless!

- Respecting that your home is a sacred trust means not using it as your private bank. I can't tell you the heartbreak I've seen when people pile up debt against their home, watch their investments or business swept away, and lose their marriages, families, and, quite literally, the roof over their heads.

- Respecting that your home is a sacred trust means only borrowing money against it with the primary purpose of improving your home, raising its value, or making it more livable.

- Respecting that your home is a sacred trust means working diligently to own it free and clear, so it becomes the cornerstone of long-term financial security. The beautiful thing about owning your home free and clear is it levels the playing field with the wealthiest of individuals because you no longer have to earn a traditional income to support your housing costs, which can run as high as 45% to 55% of your gross income.

If you make it your intention to follow the principle that homeownership is a sacred trust, I promise that you and your loved ones will be deeply grateful for many years to come.

---

* Throughout this book, all interest rates are current as of January 2019.

CHAPTER 1

FIRST-TIME HOME BUYERS—YOUR TIME HAS COME

The purpose of this book is to ignite a home buying revolution that motivates potential first-time home buyers to get out of the home rental grind and get into the homeownership game. If you are a Millennial or a Generation Y, I've written this book especially for you. With the current availability of a wide range of home financing options, we are now in the perfect storm for buying your first home. It is now easier than you might realize to responsibly buy your first home—with excellent interest rates and loan terms. I use the word, "responsibly," because, unlike during the subprime debacle, lenders today require you to verify your income and capability based on updated loan guidelines that help you qualify for attractive financing that you can afford.

A fundamental reason for writing this book is explaining how current financing guidelines open up a path to owning a home for countless individuals and couples. I want you to know about and take advantage of these guidelines. Changes made by Fannie Mae and Freddie Mac, the government agencies that buy or insure about 50% of all mortgages, have made it possible for more people to embrace the dream of homeownership. Because this news is taking time to get out, many people, especially young people, are missing out on a remarkable opportunity to experience the benefits of owning a home, including pursuing a path to financial security.

COACHING YOU TO SUCCESSFULLY BUY YOUR NEW HOME

Mortgage lending is not rocket science, but it takes determined effort to get through the steps to homeownership. My commitment is to professionally coach you through the process of buying your first home. While it is surprisingly easy to qualify for home financing, it's a very different matter to actually get your loan and close on your home without the typical drama and stress many home buyers experience.

YOU NEED A HOME BUYING STRATEGY—PERIOD

You're holding in your hands what I believe is the most valuable book you'll ever read on mortgage financing. I've packed it with insider knowledge to help you create a successful step-by-step strategy for buying your new home and ensuring that your home is a source of financial stability for decades to come.

If you enter the home buying process without a solid strategy for success, prepare for an enormous amount of stress and the real chance of heartbreak in the short-term or somewhere down the line. The process is fraught with unexpected twists and turns, and it can feel like forces beyond your control are conspiring against your goal of finding and then getting the financing to buy your new home.

"In a nutshell, if you can prove to me that you don't need a mortgage, I'll give you one."

Here are some key components of the successful home buying strategy we will explore in this book:

- Creating your personal home buying team, finding a qualified mortgage professional that you can trust, and learning the essentials of working with a knowledgeable real estate professional.

- Asking the right questions and watching out for danger signs when applying for a mortgage. I'll explain how credit scoring works, how to improve your credit report, and how a lender determines the value of your home and the size of mortgage you can afford. You'll discover that getting approved for a loan is not as hard as people often believe.

- Understanding the many types of mortgage products, why some mortgage products are better suited for your situation than others, and different strategies for qualifying for a mortgage.

- Understanding the *Tax Cuts and Jobs Act of 2017* and how it may benefit you as a home buyer.

- Learning why it's vitally important to find and work with a dedicated, experienced and qualified mortgage professional. The Wall Street Journal reported that people buying a newly built home from a builder had a 30% greater chance of getting approved for a loan than people purchasing an existing home. Why? Because the mortgage professionals working with the builder took the time to lay out a strategy to get their buyers approved. Getting a loan approved is not rocket science—if you know what you're doing.

- Using the insider knowledge that I give you to avoid being deceived by false advertising and offers too good to be true. You'll learn about the traps of adjustable rate mortgages, and how to avoid them. You'll get the secrets to securing the best competitive loan rate.

"For an explanation of the financial terms of this loan, please enroll in a continuing-education economics class at your local community college."

It's essential that you arm yourself with the knowledge that enables you to avoid making costly mistakes and to lower the stress of buying your new home. By the time you finish this book, you will know the questions to ask. And you will understand many of the answers better than some of the professionals with whom you're working!

ARE YOU PART OF THE 40%?

A survey conducted by Fannie Mae several years ago estimated that 40% of people who were renting could qualify to buy a home but did not know it! I believe this still holds true today. Think about that for a minute: 40% of people renting could be benefiting from owning a home but don't explore the possibility because they erroneously believe they don't qualify.

Lots of people have heard on the radio, read in the newspaper, and seen on TV that "you cannot get a loan" or that "money is tight." Is it any wonder that many potential first-time home buyers have stayed away from purchasing a home? Does this mean you cannot get a loan? *The answer is a resounding no!* There is often more money to lend than the lenders know what to do with.

Consider the story of Ted and Alice, a couple referred to me by a real estate professional they met at an open house. Even though they knew they couldn't qualify to buy a home, they were out on a Sunday afternoon, killing time and dreaming about having a place of their own. Ten minutes into our interview it was apparent to me that they were qualified to buy a home! After checking their credit and verifying their income, I gave them a pre-approval letter, and they were in their new home in sixty days. This type of experience was not a one-time occurrence. I see it happen all the time!

YOUNG PEOPLE AREN'T BUYING BUT SHOULD BE

In *The Atlantic*, Derek Thompson makes the observation, "This is the perfect time for many people to buy their first home, but fewer younger people are buying homes than was the case even ten or twenty years ago." He explains that "between 1980 and 2000, the percentage of late twenty-somethings who owned homes declined from 43% to 38%. The share of people in their thirties had slipped from 61% to 55% during that same period."

According to a recent Federal Reserve study, after the great recession that took place between December of 2007 and June of 2009 (National Bureau of Economic Research), the rate of young people getting their first mortgage dropped yet again. An analysis published by the National Association of Realtors in 2017 indicates that "the share of first–time buyers has declined to 34 percent, which is the fourth–lowest rate since the survey's inception in 1981." Let's explore some reasons why a lot of people who qualify to buy a home today are passing on a great opportunity.

MARRIAGE AS THE TRIGGER FOR BUYING

There are several reasons why this decline is happening, but one primary reason is pretty clear. It's the drop in the number of young people getting married or waiting to tie the knot at a later age.

In her article, *Delayed Marriage Equals Delayed Homeownership*, Mollie Carmichael writes that "traditionally, marriage has been the igniting factor in motivating people to buy a home. The rate of individuals getting married between the ages of 25 to 29 has declined by 43% between 1970 to 2013." She adds, "The housing market is unquestionably fueled by life-stage change, particularly the change of marital status and the addition or subtraction of children. These changes significantly affect where consumers want to live and what kind of home and community they will choose."

A strong case can be made that waiting until you're married to buy a home is no longer the best strategy. In a few pages, I will share a story about a client of mine, a single man in his late 20s, who got tired of paying increasingly high rent and took the leap of becoming a homeowner himself.

YOU HAVE STUDENT LOANS? YOU HAVE OPTIONS

Some analysts suggest that many young adults can no longer buy a home because of high student debt. They argue there is a correlation—and likely a causal relationship—between increased student loan debt and the decline of home-buying by young adults. As a result of the opinions of these analysts, we've seen a wave of major media articles with titles such as, *How Student Debt Crushes Your Chance of Buying A Home*, or, *College Debt is Still Keeping Grads from Buying Homes*.

In *The End of The American Dream?*, Jason N. Houle and Lawrence Berger argue that, while student debt can influence a person's ability to buy a home, it's not the primary cause of lower homeownership among young adults. For example, by 2013 the average student loan debtor owed nearly $25,000 compared to $13,000 in 1992, both in constant 2013 dollars. Their argument is that while this is certainly an increase, the higher payment is not typically a factor in determining whether student loan debtors qualify for home financing.

Consider the following: estimated student loan payments in 2013 were approximately $250 a month compared with $120 a month in 1992. This difference of $130 a month is often not material to qualifying for a mortgage. What typically hinders a person's ability to qualify is *bad debt* such as excessive credit card and auto loan debt. In the Appendix, I explain the difference between good debt and bad debt when addressing debt management. While having no debt is the best option, the key factors are the type of debt you have and how you manage it.

To understand the relative impact of other debt and student debt on qualifying for financing, let's take the example of Ken and Amy. Their total income is $68,000 a year. With no debt except a monthly student loan payment of $200, they easily qualify for a loan of $381,000. However, if their *other debt* were to rise an additional $500 a month, the loan they qualify for with conventional financing would drop to $295,000 based on the increased debt they're carrying. By other debt, we mean, in addition to their student loans, any auto loans, and credit card payments. Similarly, if their income goes up, or their debt drops again, they'd qualify for a larger loan. Just for future reference, when I refer to *conventional financing*, it means loans that are insured by Fannie Mae or Freddie Mac, the governmental agencies that buy these loans.

Having student loan debt does not, in itself, preclude you from getting home financing. The key is looking at the relationships between your monthly income, your monthly student loan payments, and your other debt payments.

UNMARRIED COUPLES OR FRIENDS QUALIFY

The conventional wisdom once was, "First comes love, then comes marriage and then comes the mortgage." This sequence is no longer the case—and hasn't been for quite a while. A 2013 study by Coldwell Banker Real Estate showed that one in four couples between the ages of 18 to 34 had bought a home before they were married, and 14% of home-buying couples who were 45 years old or older were also unmarried.

In my home financing practice, the driving force pushing unmarried couples to buy real estate is that the expense of renting is now in the same ballpark as the cost of buying. Most of my clients abhor the idea of paying rent when, with their combined income, they can easily qualify to buy a home, build equity, and become financially stable. I use the term *equity* frequently in the book, and my definition is that equity is the difference between what you owe on your home loan and the value of the property.

If you're an unmarried couple thinking about buying a home, be aware that there are some blind spots that can lead to unfortunate results without proper planning. Many unmarried couples don't realize that if their relationship splits up, the process of disposing of their property can, in some cases, actually be more complex than with a traditional divorce. The laws protecting married couples often aren't available when dealing with the financial assets of unmarried couples. Be sure to talk with your mortgage professional or a qualified attorney about these sorts of issues before buying a house. The good news is that with proper planning, owning real estate can empower and strengthen your relationship!

Groups of friends who decide to buy a home together should follow the same advice of checking with a trusted mortgage professional to develop a workable plan. One characteristic they share with most unmarried couples is that individually they can't qualify for mortgage financing, but by pooling their income and savings, they can become homeowners. But proper planning in advance of buying is a must. When buying a house with friends, I recommend you consult with an attorney who can help you draft a document that outlines the terms of your group venture to purchase a home. In this case, it is definitely true that an ounce of prevention avoids a pound of cure.

Many finance professionals discourage buying real estate unless you are married, but my belief is that, with proper planning and total transparency, both unmarried couples and groups of friends can buy real estate jointly, and effectively build wealth. I have watched numerous clients of mine, both single or unmarried couples, surprise even themselves as they quickly moved from being frustrated renters to home buyers to very happy homeowners.

SINGLES—DON'T SIT ON THE SIDELINES

Mark was single, in his late twenties, enjoying life, and working as an IT manager for a start-up. He was driven by the desire to succeed, putting in long hours at the office before spending late evenings having a good time with friends. Mark and most of his friends believed that owning a home should wait until they were married, or at least in a committed relationship.

What finally pushed Mark to rethink his perspective was that his landlord raised his rent for the fifth straight year. He arrived at my office, frustrated and angry, and resolved to do something about his situation. His rent had just increased to $1,750 a month. We calculated that if he continued renting his apartment, and his rent increased 5% each year, in five years he'd be paying $2,233 a month!

Mark had a good job, good credit, and made about $75,000 year. His biggest debts required monthly payments of $300 on his student loan, $375 on his car loan, and $150 on his monthly credit card balance of $5,000.

Mark had some savings but feared that his limited down payment funds made it unlikely he could get a loan. At the same time, if his rent kept rising, it would get even harder to save for a down payment. He was facing a *catch 22* situation, with no easy solution in sight.

Mark was also under the impression that money was tight, the loan process was complicated, and it was more difficult than ever to buy a home. He's not alone in this perception, as many people make the false assumption they can't qualify. You may be one—so please keep reading!

Mark was stunned when I showed him that with conventional financing, he could buy a home immediately with as little as 3% down—and the entire down payment could be a gift from family members. Allowing family members to gift the buyer the full amount of the down payment is a huge change in conventional financing and enables tens of thousands more people to now qualify to buy a new home. If you have little or no money for a down payment, don't despair, there are new options out there for you!

After pulling Mark's credit and looking at his pay stubs and tax returns, I qualified Mark for a home purchase of up to $252,000. In our market area, he could buy a nice condo, a strategy Mark was comfortable with due to his extensive travel schedule. He needed just $7,560 for the down payment, plus the closing costs. The total cash required to close the deal was about $14,100. Mark had $12,000 savings in the bank and felt his parents could gift him the additional funds needed for the purchase.

I decided to dig a bit deeper into Mark's situation and discovered he had just eleven months left on paying off his auto loan. He was unaware that when there are ten months or less remaining on an installment debt, as opposed to credit card debt, the lender doesn't count those payments as part of your debts. By making just one more car payment, he moved within the ten-month range and the lender deleted his $375 car payment from his total debt load. The result: Mark now qualified for a loan of $318,000, which would enable him to buy a home with a purchase price of $327,800, an increase of over $73,000. That extra bump in price gave Mark the chance to acquire a three bedroom home if he wanted.

Mark was thrilled. He decided that if he bought the three bedroom house, he could rent out two of his rooms to close friends. After collecting their rent of $850 a month each, Mark's monthly out of pocket costs for a mortgage payment of $2,568 would be just $868! This amount was a decrease in his current monthly rent payment of $882, and he could put the $882 a month difference toward paying off his student loan and credit card debts.

As you'll see shortly, Mark's story is not an outlier. He's one of many first-time home buyers who've walked through my doors believing it was a long shot to get home financing, only to discover, often in a matter of minutes, that they were in far better shape than they thought.

BEING MARRIED HAS ITS ADVANTAGES

Meagan and Paul were a newly married couple in their early thirties. Both had stable jobs, earning a total of $95,000 between them. Paul's credit was solid, but Meagan's credit was trashed because of a previous financially disastrous marriage. They were renting and unhappy that even the simplest improvements they made to their home came out of their pockets. Adding further salt to their wounds, their rent was increasing every year.

Meagan and Paul attempted to live frugally and save money by renting an apartment in a low-quality complex for $1,600 a month. They were on the third floor, there was no elevator, and climbing the stairs was a killer. They desperately wanted their own place, and unbeknownst to them, they were part of the 40% of renters who incorrectly believe they can't qualify to buy a home.

One weekend, Meagan and Mark went window shopping at open houses, not thinking they qualified for a loan but wanting to explore their dream of owning a home someday. They fell in love with a home for $410,000 and decided to stop by my office on the "outside chance" they could get some form of financing.

When I met with Meagan and Mark, they were surprised to learn there was a decent possibility of qualifying to buy the home they'd just looked at. They'd saved around $20,000 for a down payment but thought they'd need twice that much. When I did some investigating of Meagan's low credit scores, I learned her problem was some small collection accounts that her ex-husband was responsible for but never paid.

With Meagan and Paul sitting in my office, we called the five collection agencies, telling them she would pay their account to zero if they would send a letter of deletion that expunged the account and made it disappear from her credit report. Three of the five collections agencies agreed to delete the account. Within ten days, Meagan's credit score increased by fifty points! This sort of turnaround is something that frequently happens in my practice. In Chapter 4, I'll walk you through strategies for raising your credit score—in just a matter of days!

The most exciting news for Meagan and Paul was that they moved into the new home of their dreams within sixty days. Just think, in a couple of months, you could be Meagan and Paul and own your own place too!

GET IN THE HOMEOWNERSHIP GAME NOW

I love those two stories about Mark, Meagan, and Paul because they demonstrate how first-time home buyers can successfully navigate a reasonably quick path to owning a home. Their experiences provide valuable lessons worth reviewing:

- **Get in the homeownership game now:** Both single and married home buyers have learned it can be costly to wait to buy because of uncertainty about their job situation or remaining in the area. Many of my clients have realized that job changes can take months or years, and they could be paying down a mortgage, avoiding rent increases, and owning a home whose value may rise over time.

- **Renting gets more expensive:** Renters are getting frustrated because rents are going up. Based on numbers from the 2018 U.S. Census Bureau, median rents nationally have increased an average of 4.36% each year from 2012 to 2017. Many renters have been surprised to discover that a mortgage payment can be comparable to their current monthly rent payment. Also, many single buyers realize that it's relatively easy to find friends who will rent from them and help offset their mortgage payment.

- **Entire down payment can be a gift:** Current guidelines for conventional loans now allow 100% of the down payment in the form of a gift from family members. In the past, this had only been an option with Federal Home Loan Administration (FHA) financing, so it's a real game changer.

- **Down payments as low as 3%:** Buyers can get conventional financing while putting down just 3% of the purchase price of the home. To buy a median-priced home in the United

States, estimated by *Zillow* to be $231,700 in June 2018, you need a down payment of just $6,951, all of which can be a gift from a family member.

- **Low interest rates:** As interest rates continue to be near historic lows, low rates result in lower monthly payments and make it easier to qualify and get a larger mortgage.

- **Lender paid mortgage insurance:** Lenders also give buyers the option of a slightly higher interest rate rather than paying monthly mortgage insurance. This option enables many more people to qualify for financing to buy their first home.

- **High credit scores not necessary:** Meagan and Paul's case shows that credit scores don't have to be excellent to get financing. Even with a lower credit score, you can still qualify to buy your new home.

- **100% financing for Vets:** Veterans and active military have access to VA financing from the Veterans Benefits Administration that covers 100% of the purchase price, which means not needing to put any money down.

The bottom line is there are more home financing options available than ever before! By the time you finish this book, you'll know what they are and have a good idea which is the best for you!

CHAPTER 2

BUYING REAL ESTATE. A GOOD INVESTMENT?

Many people feel that buying a home is a significant investment but wonder if they'll receive the same sort of financial return they might get investing in the stock market. Let's address this concern by comparing the financial rewards of each type of investment. As you will see, a key factor to pay attention to is the amount of the initial out of pocket investment.

From 1986 to 2016, the S&P stock index grew at an annual average of 10.125% (DQYDJ, 2018). That means a $100,000 investment in the stock market in 1986 would be worth approximately $1,805,417 thirty years later.

Compare that to buying a home in 1986 for $100,000 and watching its value increase at an average annual rate of 3.6% to about $287,813. At first glance, investing in the stock market seems to be the wiser move. Let's dig deeper, as first impressions can be deceiving.

` For example, if you bought stock for $100,000, you most likely paid the entire $100,000 out of your own pocket. What about your real estate investment? If you bought a $100,000 home, your cash investment was your down payment, usually between 5% and 20% of the purchase price. Let's say your down payment was 5% or $5,000 out of pocket.

Your initial stock investment of $100,000 is now worth $1,805,417, a return on investment or ROI of about 1,805%. Your initial home investment of $5,000 is worth $287,813 today, an ROI of 5,756%—three times the ROI on your stock investment!

Some skeptics say that when calculating the ROI for the home you purchased, you should add your monthly mortgage payments as part of your investment. I would counter that, at most, you should only add the difference between what you would be paying in rent and what you're paying on your mortgage because either way, you have to live somewhere.

When you buy a house, your monthly mortgage payment may initially be somewhat higher than a rental payment for the same type of property. However, over time you will likely pay significantly less than if you were renting. And think of how much more rent you'd be paying thirty years later rather than your mortgage payments which, with a fixed rate loan, don't increase over thirty years. Any way you cut it, it's hard to argue against the wisdom of owning the home you live in.

Skeptics argue that there is no guarantee that home prices will rise. While it's true that there are no guarantees when buying a home, at a minimum you're essentially freezing the price of your home as a hedge against future price increases in housing and rent.

Regarding the matter of home values rising over time, let me briefly share two reasons why, over the long haul, home values almost always increase.

1. **Demand versus supply:** In most of the United States, the number of new houses being built is not keeping pace with population growth. As more people enter the market, the low supply in relation to the demand makes it likely that home prices will continue to climb. A 2018 report in *Global NewsWire* indicated that, "From 2000 to 2015, the U.S. fell 7.3 million units short of meeting housing demand, according to new research from the Up for Growth National Coalition, ECONorthwest, and Holland Government Affairs." Building 7.3 million additional new homes takes many years, and by the time the homes are finished, the population has expanded yet again.

2. **The cost of materials and building:** The price of construction materials like lumber continue to outpace inflation. For example, in *Builder*, David Crowe cites that the price of softwood lumber increased 26% from May 2012 to May 2013. Cities and municipalities are continually increasing fees charged to builders. Just those two factors drive up the cost of new housing. When the prices of newly constructed homes rise, as a general rule, the prices of existing homes also increase.

SHOULD I RENT OR BUY?

There are numerous reasons why it can be better to buy than to rent. Before the recent changes to the mortgage tax deduction in the 2017 *Tax Cuts and Jobs Act Tax Law*, many people believed that buying was advantageous mainly because of tax benefits. While that's one factor that made buying attractive, it's always been my perspective that there are far more persuasive reasons for buying rather than renting. Here are my top reasons for moving from being a renter to being a homeowner:

- **Build your personal wealth.** When you buy a house, your mortgage payments help you build equity and personal wealth. When you rent, your rental payments increase your landlord's wealth.

- **End the tyranny of rent increases and landlords.** The only sure thing in life besides death and taxes is that rents always increase! Once you lock in your mortgage payment, you'll be paying the same amount every month for the next 30 years while renters around you will see their monthly payments rise.

- **Watch your potential net worth grow** as the value of your home rises. According to a 2018 United States Census Bureau report, home values in the United States have gone up an average of 5.7% annually for the last five years

- **Don't get priced out of the market.** Most people's income, over time, does not keep up with increases in home prices. I encourage clients to buy as soon as they're responsibly able to because for many people, the longer they wait, the less likely they can qualify for a mortgage.

- **Independence and controlling your destiny.** You decide how to improve the property and increase the quality of life for yourself and your family.
- **A greater sense of ownership in your neighborhood and community.** Where people own the homes they live in there are higher standards of living, lower crime rates, better neighborhoods, and higher quality of life.

The bottom line is that whether you are renting or buying, you are buying real estate—but when you rent you're buying real estate for someone else! You might as well purchase the real estate for yourself.

That said, for some people there are a few good reasons, over the short-term, to rent rather than buy:

- If your credit is severely impaired and you can only get a loan with high rates and fees, it might be better to correct your credit and then buy when you qualify for better terms.
- Don't force yourself to buy a place because you've committed to a particular path. People sometimes ignore danger signs that indicate there may be issues with a property. I knew a couple who purchased a home against the advice of their real estate professional. She'd warned them about potential hidden defects the home might have. But they wanted the place, and there was no getting in their way. After they'd acquired the house, they found defects and sued the previous owner, incurred significant legal fees, and spent thousands of dollars to fix the property. Don't make their mistake.
- If a lender gives you a loan even though you have a high debt-to-income ratio, you may not have the income needed to cover your payments and can lose everything.

- If the down payment and closing costs clean out your savings and leave you with nothing to fall back on in an emergency, you may want to rent a bit longer.

While there will always be some risk in buying a new home, if you are strategic and remain open to re-evaluating your path during the home buying process, I passionately believe that owning your home is far better than renting.

BUY SOONER RATHER THAN LATER

I'm concerned when lenders and real estate professionals tell their clients to buy now to get in on rising values, and I'm uncomfortable advising clients to buy now because their home will be worth more money in the near future. It's not that home prices won't rise, but no one can honestly tell you exactly when and by how much.

I encourage my clients to buy a home as soon as they're able, mainly so they don't get priced out of the market. For me, that's the greatest concern. Most people's income doesn't keep up with increases in home prices. Clients who wait to buy wind up kicking themselves because they can't purchase the size or type of home they could have a few years before.

ONE BIG DOWNSIDE OF WAITING

Let's take a look at one of my clients. Three years ago, Jake made $63,000 a year. Now he makes $71,790. His income is rising about 4.5% a year, which, according to Trading Economics in 2018, is pretty typical over the last several years.

Three years ago, Jake considered buying a home priced at $350,000. He could make a 5% down payment of $17,500 and qualify for the necessary financing. But he was committed to making a larger down payment, so he held off to save more money.

Three years later, Jake is ready to buy, but because of a hot market, the same model of home he looked at is selling for $450,000. That's an increase of about 28.5%. Jake can no longer qualify for the needed loan. Jake's increased income is not close to keeping up with rising home prices, so to qualify to buy that same place he now needs to put 20% down. His required down payment has now ballooned from $17,500 to $90,000!

Does this mean that Jake can't buy a home? No, emphatically not! He just can't buy the home he originally wanted. While not all housing is rising as fast as my market area in Southern California, the argument remains. Over time, prices of homes almost always outpace personal incomes, not to mention one's ability to save funds for a down payment quickly.

IT'S ABOUT OPPORTUNITY COST

One valuable way to weigh the decision of whether to buy immediately or put it off for a while is something economists refer to as the *opportunity cost*. It's asking the question, "If I don't take advantage of the opportunity when it presents itself, what's the cost to me?" Let's look at opportunity cost from the perspectives of two brothers.

Both brothers earn $75,000 a year and share a similar credit score. They each recently received an inheritance of $25,000. So they're both starting from the same financial position.

Brother A decides to move forward right away and buys a home for $375,000. He uses $18,750 from his inheritance to come up with a 5% down payment. His realtor gets the seller to pay his closing costs. Because of the 5% down payment and his lower credit score, he has to pay monthly mortgage insurance which, in his case, is a wise move.

Brother B is adamant about not paying mortgage insurance or a higher interest rate because of a low down payment and holds off buying. His goal is saving up so he can put down 20% of the purchase price.

Now it's five years later. The price of that $375,000 house has increased at a 3% annual rate to $434,728, so a 20% down payment is now $86,946. That means Brother B needed to save approximately $62,000 on top of his $25,000 inheritance—an aggressive rate of $12,400 a year over a five-year period.

From an opportunity cost perspective, who made the better choice? Let's start with the cash perspective of waiting five years to buy. The following infographic shows that Brother A made the right decision, putting $28,643 more in his pocket after five years than Brother B.

CASH
Opportunity Cost of Waiting To Buy

CASH opportunity cost of buying same house now with 5% down vs. waiting 5 years to put down 20%. **$28,643**

	BUY NOW	BUY IN 5 YEARS
Home Price (3% annual price increase)	$375,000 (today)	$434,728 (5 years)
CASH OUTLAY **Down Payment**	5% DOWN $18,750	20% DOWN $86,946
Rent (5 yrs @ $1,679 a month)	$0	$100,740
Mortgage + **other owner costs** (5 yrs @ $2,522 a month)	$151,320	$0
Tax Deduction	-$11,027	$0
TOTAL CASH **OUT OF POCKET**	$159,043	$187,686

Home buyer has $28,643 more cash in pocket after 5 years.

And who made the better call from an equity perspective? Again it's Brother A with $110,565 more in equity.

EQUITY & INVESTMENT
Opportunity Cost of Waiting To Buy

EQUITY opportunity cost of buying same house now with 5% down vs. waiting 5 years.	$110,565

	BUY NOW	BUY IN 5 YEARS
Home value after 5 years (3% annual price increase)	$434,728	$0
Balance on Mortgage	$324,163	$0
TOTAL EQUITY	$110,565	$0

Home buyer has $110,565 more equity after 5 years.

Let's add up the total additional cash and equity Brother A ended up with because he took advantage of the opportunity to buy with 5% down, while Brother B waited five years to put 20% down.

For Brother B, the opportunity cost of not buying with 5% down was $139,208. The decision to delay cost Brother B a lot of money, so if the opportunity is there to buy, take advantage of it.

TOTAL CASH & EQUITY
Opportunity Cost of Waiting 5 Years To Buy

If you wait 5 years to buy the same $375,000 home you could buy today with just 5% down, this is the total cash and equity you would lose.	$139,208

Our Brother A versus Brother B example uses conservative estimates for property appreciation and interest rates. It does not factor in any quality of life issues related to homeownership versus renting. It also doesn't factor in that Brother B had to live a very frugal life and be very disciplined just to save that additional money while paying rent.

IS NOW A GREAT TIME TO BUY?

Many clients ask, "Is now the best time to buy?" Such is the eternal quest to *time the market,* to buy when prices are low and watch the value of your new home take off. If this is a question you're interested in, please read on. If not, skip to the next section.

While I advise you to think twice about timing the market, it's smart to be aware of the main factors involved in buying at the optimal time. They are:

- The supply of homes is greater than the demand
- Interest rates are low
- Financing is available

Think of each of these factors as a circle. At the intersection of the three circles is the optimal time to buy a home.

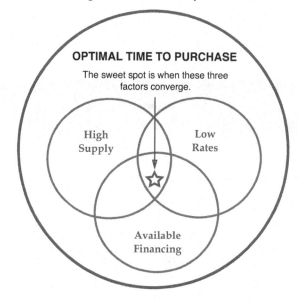

OPTIMAL TIME TO PURCHASE

The sweet spot is when these three factors converge.

High Supply

Low Rates

Available Financing

When *supply is greater than demand,* the number of sellers exceeds the number of buyers. Economists refer to this as below "equilibrium." When the market is below equilibrium, prices are typically depressed.

In the next illustration, the left side graphic provides an example of a depressed market. Five of the ten homes are up for sale.

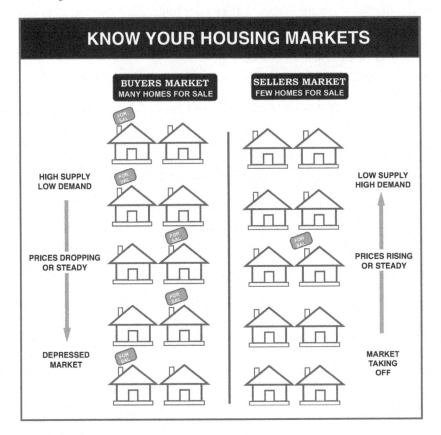

These five sellers will have to drop their asking price until the market reaches *equilibrium,* or when home prices are low enough to entice buyers to buy.

The lone seller on the right side is in a seller's market, which is when demand is high and supply is low. As a buyer, you have to navigate a seller's market carefully because purchase prices are increasing and there's lots of competition from other buyers.

Something to keep in mind is if there's a lot of new construction where you want to buy, it's not likely housing prices will drop anytime soon, and they may start rising at a good pace. When housing prices are depressed, builders stop new construction. When they believe the market is turning around, they start building. New homes coming onto the market often drive prices up even more and move an area toward being a seller's market.

When low home prices, high inventory, and low interest rates are coupled with the *availability of financing,* you have a perfect buyer's market. That said, it's important to understand the market you're considering and the inventory cycle of available homes. For instance, if there is a two-month supply of homes on the market rather than a nine-month supply, the chances are that asking prices have been rising and will continue to do so. This situation is where a knowledgeable real estate professional is invaluable. They'll have their finger on the pulse of the market in your area, know where it stands in the home inventory supply and demand cycle, and help you craft a strategy that gives you the best shot at getting your offer accepted.

BIG PICTURE THOUGHTS ABOUT OWNING A HOME

Before digging into the nuts and bolts of the home financing that you need to get a mortgage perfect for your situation, I want to offer a few big picture observations that I've shared that have been very positively received by my clients.

They cover topics such as how buying a home can be a transformative journey and not a stressful roller coaster ride; creating *conditions of satisfaction* that embody your vision of what to achieve through homeownership; and, if you're in a relationship, working as a team with your spouse or partner in managing family finances and caring for your home. These may seem like simple, obvious points, but they can make all the difference in the quality of your life as you navigate the home buying and homeownership process.

If you want to dive right into the nuts and bolts of home financing, feel free to skip the next few pages and jump forward to Chapter 3. Also, if you have specific questions about aspects of getting home financing, don't hesitate to find the section addressing your concern in the table of contents and going there. I've written this book so that the information builds naturally from one chapter to the next, but quick peaks at later sections are not only appropriate but encouraged!

HOMEOWNERSHIP AS A TRANSFORMATIVE JOURNEY

Follow the strategies in this book and you'll discover how owning a home can transform your life in many valuable ways:

- Managing your mortgage skillfully empowers you to manage all of your finances more wisely. You will experience increased financial abundance and security that benefits you in multiple ways—from your physical and mental health to the freedom it provides when you are making significant life changes.

- Owning your home can deepen your connection to your neighbors and your community because you're a stakeholder with a long-term investment who shares mutual aspirations with other homeowners.

- Owning your home can strengthen your relationship with your spouse or partner if you agree up front to make all critical decisions about your home together AND to share equal responsibility. This commitment will help you overcome strains that inevitably surface. I'll help you identify a set of conditions of satisfaction that you can make together before you even start looking for a new home.

CONDITIONS OF SATISFACTION

Whether you are single or a couple, think about setting conditions of satisfaction to follow when buying and owning your home. This concept of agreeing to conditions of satisfaction is something that my friend and mentor Scott Coady first shared with me.

There is enormous value for couples who mutually agree—even before they buy a home—to conditions of satisfaction for managing their homeownership and the outcomes they want to achieve together. Where you don't want to wind up is like the couple in the cartoon below. If you're single, setting personal conditions of satisfaction is equally worthwhile.

The best way to explain the concept of conditions of satisfaction and how they can strengthen relationships is through the stories of two couples.

Martin and Jill are like many couples who I've worked with who buy a home with the assumption that "we will never pay off this house because the mortgage is too large." A few years after they bought their home, its value increased and they were building up equity. Based on their home's increased value, Martin wanted to take out a $75,000 line of credit on their home to fund his new business. This strategy worried Jill, but she agreed to allow Martin to proceed. Five years later his business failed and they were left with a debt of $75,000 against the house—in addition to their existing mortgage.

Because the $75,000 debt was a line of credit, it was exposed to interest rate volatility, meaning that if interest rates went up, their payment on the line of credit increased. The business failure was not the main sore spot in their marriage, but taking the money out of their home equity became a huge issue because Jill felt uncomfortable with that move in the first place. The additional $75,000 in debt was not only a financial setback but emotionally damaging to their relationship.

Now let's look at Andy and Vivian. Before they bought their home, they developed a list of conditions of satisfaction. These were baseline conditions that they agreed were "chiseled in stone."

They would commit to a firm intention to pay off their home as soon as possible.

- If they received advertisements encouraging them to borrow money on their home for that "vacation they deserved" they would not hesitate to decline.
- They would keep a budget—not restrictive, but as a means to track expenses.
- They would make double principal payments—to the extent they could afford—with the goal of paying off their mortgage as soon as possible.

- They would find a financial professional to help them with their investments.

A few years after they bought their home, Andy was looking for $50,000 to start his own business. His first instinct was to take money out of the house, based on its increased value. That would be an easy option. They dismissed this temptation quickly, however, because of their previous agreement.

How would Andy raise $50,000? He set to work on a business plan, presented it to family and friends and ultimately raised the $50,000 from ten of the twenty people he spoke with—an average of $5,000 per investor. Andy's business is still a success to this day.

So what made the difference between Martin and Jill and Andy and Vivian?

- First and foremost, Andy and Vivian's commitment to not take money out of their home forced him to be creative and find other sources of money. If Andy's business failed, it would not damage his and Vivian's personal finances. Their approach shows the wisdom of keeping personal and business finances entirely separate, and of both partners making the commitment to do so.

- Martin had ready access to credit, which made it easy to go into debt without looking at other options. While Andy had to create a business plan and have it vetted by outsiders, Martin could just proceed based on his instincts. Martin and Jill are a cautionary tale in using the equity in your home for business expenditures, because if things go wrong, they can go very wrong on multiple fronts.

- Because Martin and Jill did not have an initial, clear, and firm commitment not to use home equity for business purposes, it was difficult for Jill to take a hard line, even though she had serious doubts about the wisdom of what Martin proposed. Their experience shows the importance of not making these sorts of decisions on the fly, but having a clear plan and understanding up front.

We can't know if Martin's business would have succeeded if he'd used the process Andy did, but I'm sure that Martin and Jill's relationship and their long-term financial outlook would have been much healthier and stronger if they'd agreed to a set of conditions of satisfaction up front.

CREATING YOUR CONDITIONS OF SATISFACTION

Here are five primary steps you can follow when creating your conditions of satisfaction:

1. Begin by having you and your spouse/partner each write down your own individual list of five to ten positive intentions to commit to as part of your home buying and home owning experience. Commitments such as "I want our home buying experience to strengthen our relationship and show how well we work together as a team"; "I want our house to be a warm home where we can raise our family"; "I want to own our home free and clear in fifteen years"; or, "I want us to work together to make improvements to our house so we can turn it around, sell it, make a profit, and buy a larger home."

2. Share what you've written with each other and carefully discuss each intention, so you're both entirely clear on what the other wants.

3. Create an initial conditions of satisfaction document with all the positive intentions you and your partner wrote separately.

4. Review the document to be sure you both agree to every positive intention listed. Where there is not agreement, work together to decide if that intention should be removed or reworded. Continue to discuss until every intention is something you and your partner can commit to 100%.

5. Print out your conditions of satisfaction with your list of agreed-to positive intentions. Both of you can now sign it and celebrate your shared vision and commitment.

In my experience, home buyers who agree to a clear set of conditions of satisfaction and demonstrate a commitment to protecting their home equity are more likely to reach financial security and have greater work and lifestyle flexibility over time. You only have so much life force available to create abundance for you and your family. Use your conditions of satisfaction as a compass to guide you through the ups and downs that will inevitably tempt you to abandon your commitment to seeing your home as a sacred trust and a big part of your financial security.

TWO HEADS ARE BETTER THAN ONE

From my professional experience, it makes a significant positive difference when spouses or life partners agree to be equally accountable for managing the financing and care of their home. Too often I see the unquestioned assumption that finances are primarily the man's domain. Why that stereotype still holds sway among some couples is beyond me. In today's world, it's crazy to think that a woman is not equally capable as a man of making financial decisions.

It's my observation that family finances are managed far better when both partners are involved. While one partner may more naturally take the lead on financial matters, there should still be total transparency and a sense of mutual responsibility.

Here are some thoughts to keep in mind as you move forward on your home buying and home owning adventure:

- Couples often assume that their partner is fiscally responsible, even when it's not the case. They should discuss and agree to a set of shared expectations regarding how they will spend their money and who will be the primary person managing their finances. Buying a home is an ideal opportunity to get on the same page regarding financial priorities, improved communication, and decision making.
- If you abdicate handling of finances, you give up your personal responsibility as part of a team making financial decisions together, and you place the entire burden on your partner. This situation creates an unhealthy imbalance that can lead to behavior patterns that weaken your relationship.
- One spouse may be better suited to handling the money on a day to day basis, but both spouses should be aware of how they are managing finances. I have clients where the husband

has no concept of how to handle money and the wife knows budgeting like nobody's business, but they both still know what's going on.

- Have a primary checking account in the names of both spouses and, if you do have a line of credit associated with your home, attach it to the joint account where both spouses can monitor all activity.
- Don't get personal finances and business finances mixed up. This is called co-mingling funds. Especially if you are self-employed, this can make it difficult to get mortgage financing and open you to tax audits.

THE LIBERATION OF A DEBT-FREE LIFE

A key theme running through this book is that there is enormous value in respecting your home as a sacred trust, owning your home free and clear, and living a debt-free life.

Following up on earlier thoughts about avoiding investment strategies that increase personal debt and put your home at risk, I do value the stock market and the financial rewards it can bring through prudent investing. That said, the endless cheerleading about the benefits of investing in the market need to be balanced by a discussion about the importance of reducing debt and the stability that a debt-free life brings.

As a society, we're so accustomed to carrying debt that we don't seriously consider the negative consequences. Many financial planners tout the importance of being debt-free by retirement age but also recognize the value of hitting the debt-free goal far earlier. For the average homeowner, 30% to 45% of their gross income goes to mortgage payments, with a big chunk of that paying interest.

Imagine how it would feel to be free of that burden in your forties or fifties. Think of the new adventures and experiences that would be possible if you pay off your mortgage and those funds are available sooner rather than twenty or thirty years in the future.

I have some clients who are stunt actors in the TV and film industry. You'd think they'd be the ultimate risk-takers regarding investing and financial planning. On the contrary, they're some of my most thoughtful and risk-adverse clients in these areas. If you think about it, that makes sense, given that they spend most of their time developing strategies to reduce the risk involved in the stunts they're doing. One area where they are particularly careful is in taking on any unneeded debt. In their line of work, just one misstep and their career can be over—and the last thing they want is to be saddled with debt while they're pivoting to a new line of work.

Owning your home outright, with no obligation to make monthly mortgage payments, is a significant accomplishment. Achieving this takes careful strategizing and planning. My experience is that people seldom accomplish this if they take money out of their home through refinancing or establishing a line of credit.

You have no idea of the number of couples of retirement age who I meet who are stressed because they still have to work full-time to make their mortgage payments. I don't want you to find yourself in that position, which is why I firmly believe that paying off your mortgage should be a cornerstone of your financial plan. Especially in retirement, two key factors in the quality of your life and your relationships are being debt-free and owning your home free and clear.

Having zero or minimal housing debt creates an incredible sense of freedom and financial security because, at the end of the day, one of the most important factors in a person's physical well-being is having a roof over their head—especially a roof they own!

We will discuss insider strategies for more quickly paying off your mortgage later in the book, but, for now, I encourage you to make owning your home free and clear and living a debt-free life a high priority.

Now let's get into the nuts and bolts of how to secure the mortgage that's best for you, and to do so in ways that are stress-free and enjoyable.

PART 2

KNOWLEDGE IS POWER

CHAPTER 3

THREE "C'S" OF MORTGAGE FINANCING

My goal is to position you to successfully find your dream home, secure the required financing, and make that home your own. A key factor in achieving success is understanding the three C's of mortgage financing. These are the three primary factors that lenders use to determine whether they'll give you a loan, how much they'll give you, and what the loan terms will be. Here are the three C's:

Credit: your credit scores and credit history, which lenders use to measure your intent and likelihood to repay your loan.

Collateral: the type of home you're buying, and the amount of the down payment funds.

Capability: the size of a mortgage payment you're capable of making, balanced against your income, your other debts and, in some cases, the amount of cash reserves available after your down payment.

Think of the three C's as an archway that you must pass through to get a loan approval.

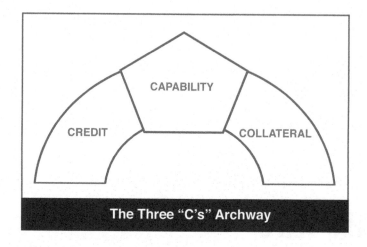

The Three "C's" Archway

On one side of the arch is your credit history and credit scores. The other is the collateral. While credit and collateral are vital aspects of assessing risk, the third C—capability—is the most important. Do you have the capability to make the mortgage payments? Do you have ample cash reserves in the event your earnings are interrupted? Capability is so important that I call it the keystone of the arch. With the keystone in place, the arch is strong, and the structure will last for a lifetime. Remove the keystone of capability and the archway collapses.

Let's pretend for a moment that you're applying for a mortgage. The first information the mortgage professional requests is your address and social security number so they can pull your credit report to assess your credit history and credit scores.

The next question is how much money you have in savings or gift money for the down payment. This money is the potential amount of cash the lender anticipates that you can contribute to your home purchase.

To determine your capability, the lender looks at your credit scores, your debt payments, the amount of your down payment, and your monthly income. All this translates into the size of a monthly mortgage payment and the corresponding loan amount the lender believes you can afford. The lender gathers all this information from your loan application, which is why it's essential to fill out the application under the guidance of a competent mortgage professional.

To best position yourself for success in buying a home, you want to optimize each of your three C's as best you can. Let's begin with your credit and determine what you want to be doing with that, starting today!

CREDIT: THE FIRST "C"

If you feel that your credit is excellent and you have a good handle on credit related issues, feel free to jump to Chapter 5 on collateral. However, if you want to learn more about the importance of credit in securing a loan and getting the best interest rate, please read on.

The English word, *credit*, comes from the Latin term, credo, which means "I believe." From the perspective of lenders, your credit-worthiness is essentially the extent to which they believe you can be trusted to repay a loan under the terms mutually agreed to. How, exactly, do they determine how much money you're qualified to borrow? One of the biggest factors is something called your credit score. The higher the score, the stronger your intent is to make your mortgage payments—at least from a lender's perspective.

OPTIMIZING YOUR CREDIT SCORE

When it comes to mortgage financing, your credit score is super important because it helps determine not only your interest rate but your required down payment and whether you can even get a loan! Your credit is vital to acquiring mortgage financing—with the best rates and terms reserved for borrowers with high credit scores.

I had a client named Sherry who wanted a conventional loan of $260,000 that carried a 3.75% interest rate and monthly payments of about $1,200. When we pulled her credit, it was worse than she realized. The best interest rate she could qualify for was 4.375%, with a monthly payment of $1,298. This rate meant she would be paying about $100 more every month than what she felt was optimal. If she were to keep this loan for ten years, her lower credit score would cost her an extra $12,000!

There was more bad news for Sherry. Not only did her poor credit result in a higher interest rate, but it made it necessary for her to earn more income to qualify for the same loan. Given Sherry's lower credit score, she would have had to make an additional $2,600 a year to get a mortgage of $260,000. Because she didn't have that extra income, she only qualified for a smaller loan that wasn't enough to buy the dream home she wanted.

Here's the exciting news—for Sherry and you! You are in control of your credit and can determine how good you want your credit to be. That's what makes this credit stuff so exciting! If you follow proven strategies, you can increase your credit score dramatically—in some cases in thirty days or less!

The model that guides the credit scoring process is designed so that the higher a borrower's credit score, the lower the risk that the borrower will default on the loan. Inversely, the lower the credit score, the higher the risk that the borrower will default. These scores range from 300 to 850.

In the infographic below you can see that as the credit score goes up, the interest rate drops!

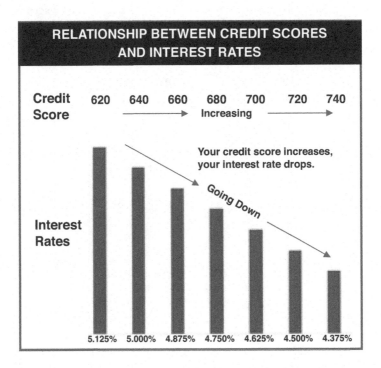

RELATIONSHIP BETWEEN CREDIT SCORES AND INTEREST RATES

| Credit Score | 620 | 640 | 660 | 680 | 700 | 720 | 740 |

Increasing

Your credit score increases, your interest rate drops.

Going Down

Interest Rates

| 5.125% | 5.000% | 4.875% | 4.750% | 4.625% | 4.500% | 4.375% |

As a mortgage professional, I've worked with people who have a net worth of $10 million and lousy credit scores. Seriously. These people have the money to pay their debts but minimal *intention* of making payments on time. I've also had clients who've never made more than $30,000 a year and would rather be dragged by wild horses than be a day late on a payment! Good character, in most cases, equals the *intent* to pay the lender back. And credit scoring helps lenders assess intent and character.

Where do you and lenders get your credit score? Something called a consumer credit bureau, the three primary ones being TransUnion, Equifax, and Experian. They are for-profit enterprises and subject to fair credit practices. The credit score that mortgage lenders request from these bureaus is known as a FICO score, which is provided by the Fair Isaacs Corporation.

"We have a complicated formula
for determining your score.
It's called the Credit Wheel of Fortune.

Every time you receive a loan or any sort of credit—in the form of a credit card or line of credit—you give your lender permission to provide credit bureaus with detailed information on the amount of your purchases and how you manage your debt. Every time any lender considers giving you a mortgage, they require your credit information in the form of a report from these bureaus. If you haven't seen your credit report before, you might be surprised at all the information being gathered about you every day. Let's take a look.

KEY COMPONENTS OF YOUR CREDIT SCORE

The key elements that influence your credit score include your payment history, credit balances, length of credit, types of credit, and new credit. This chart shows the relative weight of each component in generating your final score.

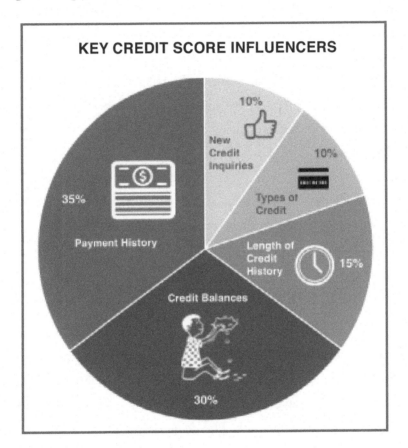

PAYMENT HISTORY: 35%

Whether you pay your bills on time carries the heaviest weight in the scoring model. Just one late payment can decrease your score by at least 25 to 50 points. The adverse effect of a late payment is reduced as time passes, up until a record of the late payment is removed, usually after seven years.

CREDIT BALANCES: 30%

This often shows up as "Balances too high," which means credit card balances are too close to the maximum allowable balance. If a cardholder owes $5,000, and the maximum allowable balance on that card is also $5,000, the scoring model records that the cardholder is maxed out on that account. If the balance is $5,200, the score is more adversely affected, because now the balance is over the limit, which can indicate the cardholder is having trouble meeting debt obligations.

The amount owed on credit accounts is so important that I've helped clients increase their scores by 70 points or more just by having them pay down their credit card balances. We'll discuss more on this shortly.

LENGTH AND DEPTH OF CREDIT HISTORY: 15%

This is the period of time an account has been open. Lenders look for the length of credit with particular creditors that appear as *trade lines* in your credit report. Trade lines are individual items that indicate an activity you have with a creditor such as a Visa credit card or a credit card from your bank. The *depth* of credit refers to the number of open credit accounts you have.

NEW CREDIT INQUIRIES: 10%

The more that potential lenders pull your credit report, the more likely there will be an adverse effect on your score. Newly opened credit accounts can also negatively affect credit scores in the short-term because the scoring model identifies that the borrower is taking on additional debt. Do not allow lenders to pull your credit report multiple times.

TYPES OF CREDIT USED: 10%

The main two types of credit are revolving credit and installment debt. Installment debt is where you are required to make a set number of payments over a predetermined repayment period such as a mortgage or auto loan, while a revolving account is a credit card.

HOW LENDERS EVALUATE YOUR CREDIT SCORES

When lenders evaluate people for a mortgage, they pull credit reports from all three credit bureaus for each person on the loan application. Here's the example of a couple named Greg and Tanya.

You can see their scores in the chart below.

CREDIT REPORT SCORES			
	Equifax	Experian	Trans Union
Greg	708	749	777
Tanya	715	752	780

Let's look more closely at Greg's credit scores:
- Equifax score = 708
- Experian score = 749
- Trans Union score = 777

Notice how Greg's scores differ based on the credit bureau. Even though all three bureaus are provided with essentially the same credit scoring algorithm by Fair Isaac, each bureau also has access to other credit information that they use to generate their credit score. The three scores are usually relatively close, and lenders use the middle of the three scores. Thus, Greg's credit report score for qualifying purposes is 749 and Tanya's is 752.

Lenders use the lowest middle score of all the borrowers to determine the interest rate. Given Tanya's middle score of 752 and Greg's score of 749, the lender will use Greg's to set their interest rate. It's worth noting that there's usually no substantial reduction in the interest rate when the score exceeds 740, so even if lenders used Tanya's score, the interest rate would be similar.

That said, if Tanya has a substantially higher credit score than Greg AND her income can qualify her on her own, it may be advisable not to have Greg on the loan and only have him on the title for the property. Before going this route, you should discuss the implications of this strategy with an attorney or CPA.

Each credit report contains specific line items that are the primary factors determining your credit score. These are referred to as *US FICO Score Reason Codes*. Here are some examples of codes that may show up on your credit report:

- 08 - Too many inquiries last twelve months
- 12 - Length of time revolving account have been established
- 11 - Amount owed on revolving accounts is too high
- 21 - Amount past due on accounts

Be aware that the credit scoring process works primarily on negative feedback, so adverse credit information carries much more weight than positive credit information. That's why if you're trying to improve your credit score, a significant focus should be clearing out negative credit.

Right now I'd say our biggest asset is our credit card debt.

TRENDING DATA

Many of the rules described above for maintaining an excellent credit score are weighted towards *when* you pay your bills. In other words, if I pay all my bills on the 29th day of each month it's possible that I will have the same credit score as someone paying their bills when due—typically the first of the month. Even if I end up with late fees for paying beyond the due date, there will be no impact on my credit score. I have been able to play the system and still keep a good to excellent score.

However, please be aware that this set of rules is changing due to the recent development of something called "Trending data." Trending data not only measures *when* you pay your bills but *how* you pay your bills. This is a crucial change in the evolution of credit scoring and includes factors such as:

- Do I pay my balances to zero each month?
- Do I pay my bills on the due date or do I incur late fees?
- Do I pay down my balances on a regular basis below the previous month's balance?
- Are my outstanding balances trending up or down?
- Do I only make the minimum payments?

These new criteria view your credit data as trending over twenty four months rather than the current method of being a snapshot in time. The key point is to take all the above criteria into consideration when managing your credit and making payments.

UPSIDE OF SPREADING CREDIT RISK

Is using two credit cards with lower balances better than using one credit card charged to the maximum balance? The answer is "Yes!!" Instead of maxing out one credit card for $5,000, simply carry a balance on two credit cards for $2,500 each, with a maximum allowable balance on each card of $5,000. By using this method, believe it or not, you will have a higher credit score. It sounds crazy, but more credit that is *paid as agreed* gets you a higher score. One important factor to remember is that having a balance of 50% or less of the maximum allowed on your credit card helps you maintain a higher credit score. The lower your credit balance in relation to your maximum available balance, the more positive effect it has on your credit score.

When it comes to your credit score, think for a minute about why there is less risk when you spread $5,000 across two accounts. If you have one account for $5,000, and you default on the payment, you are at a 100% default rate. However, if you have two accounts and default on one account you have a 50% default rate. This spreads the risk over a greater number of cards. You have more cushion in an emergency. If you have three or four credit cards with balances below 50% of the maximum limit, the scoring model will calculate a higher score.

SCORE VARIATION BETWEEN CREDIT BUREAUS

When there is inconsistency in your credit scores from the three credit bureaus, it's usually because they don't have all the same information on your credit profile. For example, a lender may report a collection account to Equifax but not report to Experian or TransUnion. In that case, your Equifax credit score could be much lower than the other two scores. The reality is that many lenders are regional, and they report information only to the credit bureau that is dominant in their region. Collection agencies often do the same, so the credit bureaus wind up working with different data sets. This is why mortgage lenders will want to see all three credit bureau reports.

YOUR CREDIT SCORE MAY BE HIGHER WHEN YOU PULL IT

I'm often asked, "Why are my credit scores when I pull my credit through the credit bureaus, different than the scores when I apply for a mortgage?" The answer is that the credit score you receive directly from the bureaus may not be the same scoring model used by your mortgage lender. All mortgage lenders require FICO credit scores from Fair Isaacs Corporation . However, the scores from the bureaus use a credit-scoring model called VantageScore, which they have developed themselves. The problem is that the VantageScore model is newer than the FICO model and mortgage lenders aren't as confident in its ability to predict risk. While the VantageScore and FICO scoring models are similar, with scores ranging from 300 to 850, the mathematical algorithms used to arrive at the actual scores are different. As a result, the scores you receive will be different because of the two scoring models.

When you use a different score than what your lender uses it can mislead you into believing your credit is acceptable for a mortgage loan! This happened with a client of mine who showed me a printout of his VantageScore at 754, which is terrific. When I pulled his FICO score, it was 680 which meant he couldn't qualify for the interest rate he was expecting on his mortgage.

If all of this background information on credit scores seems overwhelming, hang with me. There is great news coming. In the next chapter, I am going to show you how to improve your credit in as little as two weeks. Plus, throughout the book, I will brief you on *Home Ready* and *Home Possible* sponsored by Fannie Mae and Freddie Mac. In many cases, these programs will give you the edge for better rates and terms, especially if you have credit challenges. For example, your credit score could be as low as 680, and you might still get the same rate as if your score was 740! That's an improvement in rate of 375%! This can mean that in some cases your score can be as low as 620 and you'll still get greatly improved pricing compared to standard pricing guidelines. Please note, however, that these programs can have income limits and property location restrictions. So it's essential to work with a knowledgeable mortgage professional who can help you determine if these programs are possible options for you.

Now let's look at strategies for correcting your credit and raising your score! If your credit is perfect, you can jump forward to Chapter 5.

CHAPTER 4

RAISING THAT CREDIT SCORE

When you first look at your credit report, there's a good chance you may not like what you see. Maybe you were penalized for a late payment that you're sure is an error, or you discover a credit card under your name that you never applied for. The good news is that whatever the damage to your credit, there are ways to correct it.

That said, let me share something with you that may hurt your feelings: *The three consumer credit bureaus we just discussed—they don't care about you.* Sorry if your feelings have been hurt, but this information needs to be out in the open!

If you think the credit agencies care about you as a consumer, give them a call and ask to speak with someone. Good luck! They have a better web of voice transfers than the IRS. Their phone system is designed to do everything possible not to transfer your call to a live person.

The bottom line is that you are not their primary customer—the banks and lenders are. The only reason they respond to you—usually by mail—is because of laws imposed by Congress.

You may have heard that credit bureaus are required to show a late payment on your credit report for seven years. That's incorrect. Under fair credit reporting, the law states it CAN stay on your report for seven years, meaning it CAN be removed sooner if the creditor agrees. The lenders, however, have agreements with credit bureaus on what they can and can't remove from your credit report and the time frames for doing so. Lenders use the maximum time limits allowed by law before deleting any derogatory credit. This approach makes sense for credit bureaus and lenders who want to keep the integrity of the credit reporting system in check, but can inappropriately hurt someone who makes a simple mistake.

For example, if you keep your credit immaculate and always make your payments on time, while a friend of yours often makes his payments late, it wouldn't be fair if you both ended up with similar scores just because he's always asking his creditors to remove derogatory information. On the other hand, if you inadvertently make a single late payment, why should you be penalized by having it on your credit for the next seven years? That's why it's critical to work with a mortgage professional who knows what they're doing.

I've found great success by following these simple steps: identify the problem, correct your credit now, and rescore your credit. Let's examine each of them in detail.

IDENTIFY THE PROBLEM

If you have excessive debt or derogatory or impaired credit, figure out what aspect of your credit, when changed, will most likely increase your credit score. A good mortgage professional has access to predictive software that's capable of generating a projected future credit score based on changes you make to your credit profile. Without this tool, figuring out where to focus your credit repair efforts can be like trying to hit a bull's-eye while blindfolded.

After you identify any problems, your mortgage professional can determine which strategies can increase your score. Where most consumers fail is in cleaning up past late payments that won't come off the report any time soon or won't have a sizable impact on the score.

There are three things you can do to increase your credit score dramatically. The first is to delete derogatory accounts such as collection accounts and the like. The second is to pay down your balance on each credit account to less than 50% of the maximum allowable credit. The third is to pay off any recent collection accounts.

CORRECT YOUR CREDIT—NOW

The most dramatic effect on your credit score is getting derogatory accounts deleted. In many cases, the original account was written off by a lender when they sold it for pennies on the dollar to a collection agency. While not all collection agencies or creditors will remove the account when paid in full, it's worth the effort, especially if the collection account should not have been there in the first place. Some derogatory accounts are easier to delete than others. The most difficult are those from large banks and credit card companies, while the easiest are collection accounts for items like past due medical bills. The creditor's objective is getting you to pay the outstanding balance, not keeping it on your report.

"Your credit score is a bit low but we can still offer you a loan. Do you have a problem being fitted for an electronic ankle cuff?"

Wherever possible, pay off *recent* collection accounts that have appeared on your report in the last year. This will almost always improve your credit score. In some cases, it may not be wise to pay off old collection accounts, because that action may actually reduce your score. This is because paying on an old collection report actually makes it appear to be recent on your credit report. The bureaus then lower your score because they see what seems to be recent collection activity. So check with your mortgage professional before paying off past collection accounts.

RESCORING YOUR CREDIT

There is a process called a *rapid rescore* that mortgage professionals can perform that enables you to get a higher credit score within a matter of days, something you'll want to take advantage of before submitting your application to a loan underwriter.

Let's first look at how the rescoring process relates to strategies covered in our last section. This includes deleting derogatory accounts, paying down credit card and loan balances, and paying off collection agencies. As a standard practice, after you've paid off your balances on derogatory accounts, the original creditor contacts the three primary credit bureaus and sends a letter of deletion that shows you've taken corrective action. It can take as long as two months for this information to cycle through all three credit agencies. The good news is there's a faster way.

As a mortgage professional, I can take your letters of deletion from the creditor or collection agency and send them to my credit vendor, who has direct access to the three credit bureaus. They send your letters of deletion electronically to all three bureaus and, in five to fifteen days, the changes that you've put in place have been recorded. Our credit vendor tells us when the changes are made and we re-pull your credit report, generally with a higher score— sometimes as much as 80 points higher!

As part of the rapid rescore process, consider paying down credit card debt or outstanding loans you have. Paying off excess debt will get you a higher credit score and help qualify you for a larger loan and a lower interest rate. If you can pay down debt before applying for your mortgage, the rescore method is perfect for you.

That strategy is what a client of mine named David did. He had $10,000 in credit card debt to pay off to qualify for the loan he wanted. He paid off all his credit card balances, and I sent his letters to my credit vendor who then notified all the bureaus. Seven days later we received word that everything had cleared. When I pulled his credit report, all his balances now showed zero and his credit score jumped forty-five points, enough to get a lower interest rate.

While some lenders tell you it takes one to two months for your credit score to be updated, if you work with a knowledgeable mortgage professional and use the rapid rescore method, you can get an updated score within five to fifteen days.

I'm not a big fan of most credit repair agencies because too often I've seen them take money from clients and not get any results. Some legitimate credit repair agencies follow key rules, such as not charging up front except for initial counseling fees and only billing when they get results. Please avoid any agencies who don't follow those basic guidelines. You're better off moving forward, paying down balances, and taking the other actions I've described, rather than working with credit repair agencies to clean up old credit issues.

QUICK SUMMARY—IMPROVING YOUR CREDIT REPORT

We've covered a lot of options for improving your credit, so here is a quick summary of the key actions you can take.

- Your creditor is the bank or credit card company that advanced you money via a loan, credit card, or line of credit.
- Credit bureaus use the information provided by your creditors and your FICO score to create your credit report. They share this information with lenders who use it when deciding whether to approve your mortgage.
- By working with your creditors and the credit bureaus, you can significantly improve your credit score and position yourself to get better loan terms.
- When you get your credit report, identify derogatory accounts and develop a strategy for paying off accounts you still owe.
- Ask past creditors to remove incorrect or derogatory information.
- When paying off derogatory accounts or reducing loan balances, get proof you paid and request a letter of deletion.
- After doing the above, have your mortgage professional do a rapid rescore, which should show a higher credit score to share with lenders who are considering giving you a loan.
- DO NOT run up additional credit charges or add new credit accounts while in the home buying process. Lenders recheck your credit report right before funding your loan. If your credit score drops or you have additional debt, they may pull back on the financing.
- Do not allow your credit to be pulled by multiple lenders.

CHAPTER 5

COLLATERAL—THE SECOND "C"

We've built the first side of our home buyer's arch with credit, and we're now ready for the second side of the arch, which is the collateral.

There are two basic types of loans that lenders make to consumers. You likely have experience with one type, a signature loan, the most common being a credit card. A signature loan is based on your credit history and your promise to repay it per mutually agreed terms. This type of loan is the money you borrow when you use a credit card to purchase something.

The other primary lending method is a collateralized loan. A collateralized real estate loan uses property that has financial value as security against the loan. From the lender's perspective, they want the property you're using as collateral to have greater value than the amount of money they're lending in the form of a home mortgage. The genius behind collateralized home mortgages is they enable lenders to give you a much lower rate than loans that aren't secured against the property.

When buying a home, the lender requires that the loan they're giving you be collateralized by the property you are buying. When you sign the note that promises repayment of the loan, you also sign a *trust deed* or a *mortgage note*, depending on the state in which you live. This action attaches the note to the property, so it becomes the collateral. The county recorder then records the trust deed or mortgage. In the event of non-payment and default on the mortgage, the lender can take your home, an action known as foreclosure.

Let's look at the different types of properties you can use for collateral and how lenders treat each of them.

SINGLE-FAMILY HOMES

Lenders view a single-family home as the best form of collateral. They have the lowest risk of default for a couple of reasons:

- Pride of ownership is higher for single-family homes.
- The owner has complete control over the property and tends to maintain it better because they can manage every aspect of home care.

If you're only interested in buying a single-family home, skip the next few sections on condominiums and other types of residential property and go directly to Chapter 6.

MODULAR HOUSING

A modular home is assembled on the property. In other words, it's brought in pieces and put together like Legos™. It's usually built on a permanent foundation.

There is one hitch: the lender treats modular homes differently than regular single-family homes, and looks at the value of other modular homes in the market area in assessing the value of the home you're buying. If there are no other modular homes in the area, the lender uses conventional homes as comparables but may adjust the value of the home. Based on the lender you are working with, there may be a slight difference between modular homes and single-family residences as far as interest rate, qualifying, or down payment requirements.

MULTI-UNIT PROPERTIES

These can be a duplex, triplex or four-plex, or, respectively, two homes, three homes, or four homes joined into one building. They can be separate units as long as they're on the same lot. Most lenders don't have issues with these properties, especially if the owner occupies one of the units. They find it reassuring if the borrower is an onsite owner who can take care of repair problems.

This can be an excellent way to go with your first home. I had a client who bought a triplex with great financing based on it being an owner-occupied residence. He lived in one of the units and rented out the other two. The rent from the two residences covered his entire mortgage payment, so he lived in his unit at no cost while using the renters' payments to pay his mortgage. That's a pretty sweet deal!

CONDOMINIUMS AND TOWNHOMES

The popularity of condominiums and townhomes has exploded due to the relatively high prices of single-family residences. Consequently, a large population of home buyers who are priced out of the single-family house market can still purchase a condominium or townhome. They can come with a range of amenities such as swimming pools and tennis courts, and owners don't have to worry about yard work and other types of property maintenance.

To keep things simple in this section, I'm just going to refer to condominiums, with the understanding that, in many cases, the same factors apply to townhomes. There is one important caveat: not all townhomes are legally designated as condominiums. Rather, they appear on county records as a *planned unit development*, commonly referred to as a PUD. This distinction is important for two primary reasons:

- If you are seeking FHA financing, all condominiums must be approved by FHA. This approval is not required with a PUD.
- There are no pricing hits or increased rates if the property is designated as a PUD.

Consequently, if you're looking at a particular townhome, be sure to ask if it's legally designated as a condominium or a PUD.

The following story about a client of mine named Denise shows how condominiums provide many people with the opportunity to become first-time home buyers. Denise came from a family who had rented and had never owned their home. When we reviewed her financial information, she didn't qualify for the mortgage needed to buy a single-family home in our market area. But she had a real passion for becoming a homeowner, and that's where buying a condominium came into play. We got Denise the financing to purchase a studio condominium for $135,000. Now she's the first proud homeowner in her family and, rather than renting, she's paying down her mortgage and building up equity.

A Homeowners Association (HOA) manages condominiums and are responsible for all exterior maintenance of the complex, from painting the buildings to landscape maintenance. If you buy a condominium, you will typically pay between $250 to $500 a month in fees to the HOA, with the average being about $350/month. The higher priced projects usually carry the higher HOA fees.

There are some increased risk factors for lenders when loaning money to condominium buyers. Unless you put down at least 25%, they are likely to increase the interest rates for condominium financing compared to rates for single-family homes. For example, if an interest rate of 4.375 for a single family residence may jump to between 4.50% and 4.625% for a condominium. On a $275,000 loan, that's an increase of at least $41 a month on your mortgage payment. There are, however, exceptions to this based on the loan program. As previously noted in chapter 3, if you meet the guidelines for *Home Ready* or *Home Possible*, the rate increase for a condo can be eliminated. Please be sure to consult with your mortgage professional to determine if you can take advantage of these programs.

When looking at condos, carefully consider the quality of the construction and the ongoing maintenance of both the unit you're looking at and the condominium complex. A well-built condominium can be a great value because of all the resources that are available to you, but if the condo project was not well constructed or is not well managed it can be a real nightmare.

I can't emphasize the following point too much: always make certain that your lender or a mortgage professional orders the HOA certification on the condominium as soon as escrow opens or your home is in contract. You don't want to go through the entire loan process and then, in the end, have the lender receive the HOA certification and not approve financing based on issues like pending litigation.

MANUFACTURED HOMES

Most lenders consider a manufactured home to be the same as a mobile home without wheels, even though most of them are driven onto the property on wheels. The "on wheels" bit is the killer issue. While it may be required to secure the unit to the foundation, the lender's concern is that if it came in on wheels, it could leave on wheels. To get a mortgage on a manufactured home, the buyer must own or will own, the land upon purchase of the home.

The quality of many manufactured homes has come a long way, and some provide relatively deluxe living environments with many amenities. Be sure to buy a manufactured home built after June 15, 1976, when standardized regulations were instituted that resulted in homes that are safer and better built. Most lenders no longer provide loans for manufactured homes built before those new rules went into effect.

If the manufactured home is in a mobile home park, it's not considered real estate and, in most states, is under the jurisdiction of the DMV. Some lenders do specialize in providing financing for these homes. If you're looking to buy a manufactured home, FHA loans and VA loans for military veterans offer some of your best options.

SAFE TO RISKY COLLATERAL

Lenders are concerned both with the type of property you use for collateral and how you plan to use the property. There are three main classifications, each with a level of risk set by lenders:

- Primary residence—least risky
- Second homes—moderately risky
- Investor properties—most risky

"Where I come from it's called collateral."

PRIMARY RESIDENCE

From a lender's perspective, the best collateral is a property intended to be the primary residence of the buyer. It's the lender's preferred collateral for many reasons, especially because people who own the home they live in have a natural pride of ownership—a very powerful force. This factor is such a big deal to the lender that they'll give you better loan terms on a property that will be a primary residence and not a rental.

SECOND HOMES

If you declare that the property you're buying is a second home, you must be able to qualify for two mortgage payments. Individuals in the income stratum inclined to have second homes usually qualify for this extra debt. Second homes have many of the same mortgage rates as a primary residence.

INVESTMENT PROPERTIES

Investment properties carry the highest risk of foreclosure, so your lender will usually ask for a higher down payment, at least 20% to 25%, and give an interest rate that is at least a half a point higher than for a primary residence.

INTEREST RATES VARY WIDELY

Because interest rates can vary based on the type of collateral you have, always work with a qualified mortgage professional who can help you find a lender whose mortgage terms best fit your collateral, your needs, and your plans.

CHAPTER 6

YOUR DOWN PAYMENT IMPACTS YOUR LOAN TERMS

We've just looked at different kinds of collateral, and how they influence the mortgages terms you can get. Now let's look at a formula that lenders use called *loan-to-value* (LTV). Lenders use the LTV to help evaluate risk and determine how much they'll loan you and how much you'll need as a down payment.

The LTV is a simple formula by which you divide a loan amount by either the purchase price or the appraised value of the house you want to buy. If the appraised value is lower than the purchase price, lenders divide by that amount.

Let's see how the formula works when using the purchase price. If the house has a purchase price of $375,000 and you want a loan for $300,000, divide the $300,000 loan amount by the $375,000 and you get an LTV of 80%. Here's the basic formula.

LOAN TO VALUE FORMULA (LTV)		
LOAN AMOUNT	$300,000	
PURCHASE PRICE	$375,000	= 80% LTV

The next step is understanding that, to make up the difference between the purchase price of $375,000 and a loan of $300,000, you need to make a down payment of $75,000. This illustration shows the elements involved in buying a $375,000 house with an LTV of 80%.

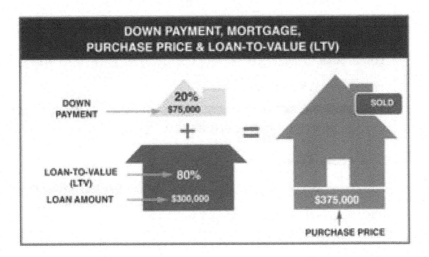

ADDING YOUR CREDIT SCORE INTO THE LTV EQUATION

Let's say you have a credit score of 740. The lender says they'll offer you an interest rate of 4.375% based on an LTV of 80%. That means they'll loan you 80% of the $375,000, or $300,000 if you make a down payment of $75,000 to cover the total purchase price.

If you can make a 10% down payment, that bumps up your LTV to 90%. The higher LTV means the lender will charge you a higher interest rate or give you the same rate but require mortgage insurance, an area we'll cover shortly.

As the infographic below shows, a key factor that you control is the size of your down payment. The down payment directly impacts the LTV, the size of the loan, your interest rate, and your monthly payment.

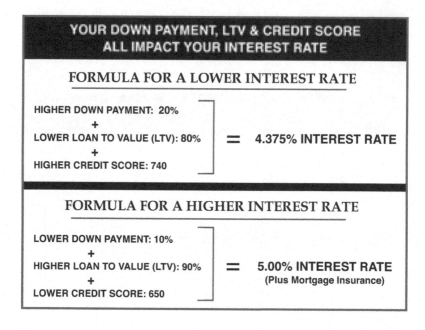

The bottom line is that the lower your LTV and the higher your credit score, the better terms you will get on your mortgage financing.

HOME APPRAISALS AND LOAN-TO-VALUE

When lenders consider giving you a mortgage, they want the property you're putting up as collateral to be appraised to determine its value. The lender retains an appraisal management company (AMC) who assigns an independent appraiser.

Under Federal guidelines instituted after the subprime mortgage debacle, your lender no longer has direct access to the appraiser. After the AMC selects an appraiser, it is usually the listing agent who meets them at the property, gives them access, and provides information to support the purchase price. The appraiser can choose whether or not to accept such information.

Back in 2005, this place
was worth $850,000.

Lenders require appraisals to protect themselves from financing overvalued properties. They consider a range of factors, including the condition of the property and, most importantly, recent sales of comparable homes in the area. The appraisal is provided both to the buyer and the lender.

In many cases, determining an accurate appraised value for a property is an art as much as a science. I was involved with a property with a purchase price of $650,000. Another lender was handling the financing, and an appraiser from outside the area gave it a value of $580,000. The real estate professional involved knew the appraisal was off-base and asked if I could help. We agreed to select a new lender and ordered a new appraisal.

As a mortgage professional, I'm not permitted to participate in choosing an appraiser, but the one who was assigned knew the market area intimately. The property was valued at $650,000. Because of the listing agent's knowledge of the local market we knew the out of town appraiser was off base and had the appraisal value corrected— to the benefit of both the seller and the buyer.

THE APPRAISED VALUE IS LOWER. UH OH.

If the appraised value of the home is lower than the proposed purchase price, the lender uses the appraised value to determine the LTV. This affects the size of a loan, the loan terms, and the amount of the required down payment.

Judy and Ed were a couple considering buying a home with a purchase price of $450,000. At an LTV of 80%, the lender would loan them $360,000, so they'd need a down payment of $90,000. Unfortunately, the appraised value came in at $400,000, not $450,000. The low appraisal put Judy and Ed in a tight spot because their lender required an LTV of 80% and would loan them only $320,000 based on the $400,000 appraisal. Judy and Ed would have to make up the difference—an additional $40,000 on top of the $90,000 down payment they anticipated.

Judy and Ed pursued three different options. First, they negotiated with the seller to reduce the purchase price to the appraised value but got no traction. Second, they asked the lender to agree to a higher LTV which reduced the size of their down payment. The lender agreed to a higher LTV, but only if Judy and Ed purchased mortgage insurance or accepted a higher interest rate. Third, their real estate professional worked with the listing agent to present information to the appraiser that argued for a higher value, but the appraiser held his ground.

In the end, the seller lowered the purchase price by $25,000, and Judy and Ed made a down payment of $105,000 and hit the LTV of 80% required by the lender.

When there is high demand and rising home values, the appraised value may be *lower* than the purchase price because a key metric in appraisals is the sales prices of comparable homes in the area during the previous two to four months. In this scenario, buying a home at a purchase price higher than the appraised value may be the wisest course, even if that means making a larger down payment or having a higher LTV.

"And this is the downstairs half-bath."

Sometimes properties are appraised at a *higher value* than the purchase price. This higher value does not, unfortunately, help the borrower. Lenders are mandated to follow the rule of conservatism and always use the lower number, so they use the purchase price and not the higher appraised value in determining the LTV.

MORTGAGE INSURANCE AND SHARING THE RISK

We previously touched on the fact that lenders require home buyers to buy mortgage insurance, often referred to as MI, if they can't cover a 20% down payment. MI is an insurance policy that helps cover lenders if you default. If you're buying a $100,000 property and have a $10,000 down payment, the lender will loan you $90,000. That's 90% of the purchase price and an LTV of 90%. If you default, the MI policy kicks in and the lender is paid additional funds to cover their loss. In essence, the insurance protects the lender, giving them the same risk exposure as an 80% LTV!

You pay the mortgage insurance company a monthly premium for this policy. When you get your monthly mortgage bill, it includes both your mortgage payment and your MI premium payment. Various factors determine the amount of your MI payment, including the size of your down payment, your credit score, and the type of loan for which you've applied.

The less money you put down, the higher your MI premium. You can see this principle in the following infographic where, based on a 680 credit score, if you put down 15% your monthly MI payment is just $85 a month but if you put down 3% your monthly MI jumps to $424!

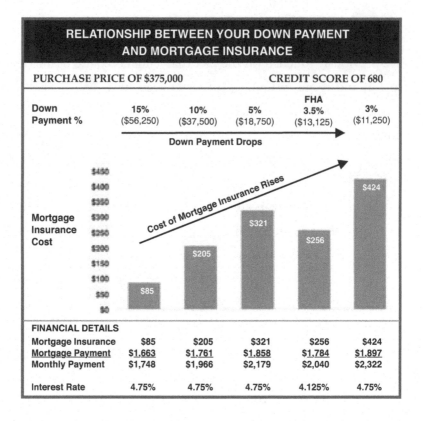

RELATIONSHIP BETWEEN YOUR DOWN PAYMENT AND MORTGAGE INSURANCE

PURCHASE PRICE OF $375,000 — CREDIT SCORE OF 680

Down Payment %	15% ($56,250)	10% ($37,500)	5% ($18,750)	FHA 3.5% ($13,125)	3% ($11,250)

FINANCIAL DETAILS

Mortgage Insurance	$85	$205	$321	$256	$424
Mortgage Payment	$1,663	$1,761	$1,858	$1,784	$1,897
Monthly Payment	$1,748	$1,966	$2,179	$2,040	$2,322
Interest Rate	4.75%	4.75%	4.75%	4.125%	4.75%

You should also be aware that the higher your credit score, the lower your *MI* payment. For example, if your score increases from 680 to 740, your monthly MI payment will drop from $424 to $227! Additionally, this is where I encourage you to ask your mortgage professional about the Home Ready or Home Possible financing. If this is an option, you will most likely see an additional reduction in your MI.

Now for some good news! With a conventional loan, you're only required to carry your MI policy for two years. After that, you can petition to have your MI removed, based on how much you've paid down on your original loan, which likely will require a significant cash infusion on your part. You can also petition based on how much the appraised value of your home has increased. Your mortgage professional can outline strategies to help you with this. If you get an FHA loan, be aware that, in most cases, the MI stays with the mortgage the entire life of the loan. Unlike with conventional financing, you cannot remove it. The only way you can get rid of the MI is refinancing your loan.

Eliminating your MI premium is something you want to do. A client named Rudy was buying a $250,000 home and was prepared to make a 10% down payment. We qualified him for a 30-year fixed loan at 4.25%, a pretty good rate at the time. His monthly mortgage payment was $1,107. The lender required MI with a monthly premium of $175, so his total monthly payment was $1,282. Because of the cost of the MI, his effective interest rate wound up around 5.53%, so Rudy committed himself to make his MI go away after two years!

It's worth noting that not all MI is created equal. Please check with the lenders you are considering and get their MI rates, as they can vary by 20% or more!

LENDER PAID MORTGAGE INSURANCE

An attractive option that many of my clients choose is lender-paid mortgage insurance (LPMI). The main reason to go with LPMI is that you'll wind up paying a real interest rate that is, in many cases, much less than what you'd get with traditional MI. For instance, in the infographic on the next page, a homeowner with a credit score of 740 gets an effective interest rate of 4.75% with LPMI rather than a real rate of 4.945% with MI. On a home loan of $337,500, that's an extra $39 a month in your total mortgage payment that adds up over the years. Another benefit of LPMI is potential tax benefits that include writing off the interest expense. Please see the section titled

The Tax Cuts & Jobs Act of 2017 and the *Mortgage Interest Deduction* in Chapter 7 for details.

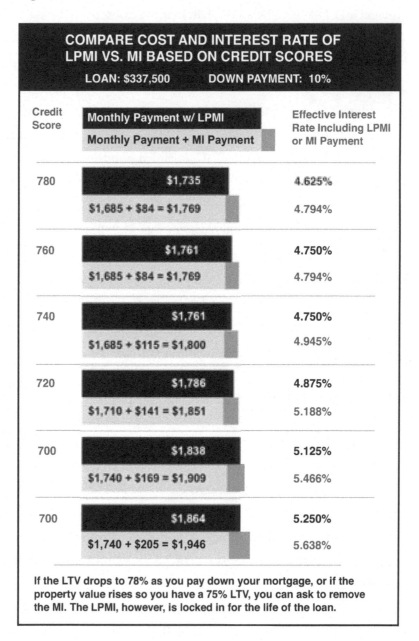

COMPARE COST AND INTEREST RATE OF LPMI VS. MI BASED ON CREDIT SCORES

LOAN: $337,500   DOWN PAYMENT: 10%

Credit Score	Monthly Payment w/ LPMI / Monthly Payment + MI Payment	Effective Interest Rate Including LPMI or MI Payment
780	$1,735	4.625%
	$1,685 + $84 = $1,769	4.794%
760	$1,761	4.750%
	$1,685 + $84 = $1,769	4.794%
740	$1,761	4.750%
	$1,685 + $115 = $1,800	4.945%
720	$1,786	4.875%
	$1,710 + $141 = $1,851	5.188%
700	$1,838	5.125%
	$1,740 + $169 = $1,909	5.466%
700	$1,864	5.250%
	$1,740 + $205 = $1,946	5.638%

If the LTV drops to 78% as you pay down your mortgage, or if the property value rises so you have a 75% LTV, you can ask to remove the MI. The LPMI, however, is locked in for the life of the loan.

Be aware that if you go with LPMI, you can't petition to drop the rate after two years. The only way to get rid of LPMI is to do a total refinance and get a lower rate when you qualify. Just as was the case with MI, with *Home Ready* and *Home Possible* financing options there can be a reduction in LPMI rates.

Some of the advantages of standard MI are:

- You can petition to remove it after two years, based on rapid appreciation or it will automatically drop off after the LTV hits 78%. This usually takes eight to ten years based on the amount of your initial down payment.
- MI works well for credit scores down to 620. FHA also allows for scores as low as 580. On an exception basis, FHA guidelines even allow for credit scores below 580. However, there are additional guidelines and terms, so check with your mortgage professional.
- MI provides for greater loan availability among lenders.

Some financial planners believe that the downside of paying MI or LPMI is so great that you should only buy a home when you can put down at least 20%. I do not subscribe to that philosophy and will explain why shortly.

MAKING THE DOWN PAYMENT

Perhaps the biggest single challenge of buying a home is coming up with the down payment. While most people can qualify to make the monthly mortgage payments, saving for the down payment can be difficult.

If you go for a conventional home loan, have good credit and income, and can make a down payment of 20%, most lenders will approve your loan. If you don't have that 20% to put down, don't despair, you have options. As previously noted, based on your loan amount, there are loan programs that require down payments as low as 3%. FHA financing is especially useful as only 3.5% is required for the down payment, while still allowing for larger loan amounts. This comes in handy if you live in a high-cost county.

VA financing for veterans covers up to 100% of the sales price on loans up to $726,525 as of 2019, depending on the county where the loan is originated. Check with your mortgage professional for details on loan limits in your county.

Clients always ask what factors to keep in mind when deciding how much to put down on a house. Here are my key factors:

- Start by finding out the minimum down payment a lender will require, based on your income and credit, to qualify you for the loan amount you want. That's the bottom line for being in the game.
- Balance the size of the down payment you can make against the amount of the mortgage payment you're prepared to pay. You may qualify for a larger loan with higher monthly payments than you're comfortable with. One way to reduce those monthly payments is to make a larger down payment.

- There are closing costs when finalizing the purchase of your new home. These run in the thousands of dollars, and you must pay them from your available cash. Some clients ask if they can roll closing costs into the loan amount. The answer is no. Closing costs can't be included in the loan and are above and beyond your down payment. There are strategies we address later for mitigating the closing costs you pay out of pocket.

- With some conventional loans, lenders may require you to have cash in the bank to cover at least two mortgage payments.

- Once you've estimated your closing costs, calculate what that leaves you in cash for home repairs. If the home is in great shape or will be after the current owner makes repairs, you may not need much money for this expense.

- Your final equation is calculating the advantage you gain if you put more money down, resulting in a lower LTV, and, thus, a lower interest rate and lower monthly payments.

DON'T LET A SMALL DOWN PAYMENT GET IN YOUR WAY

Some financial professionals believe you shouldn't buy a home unless you can put down 20%. Their concern is if you put down less you then have to pay mortgage insurance. Additionally, they worry that your mortgage payment may be too large or too high of a percentage of your overall income. These are legitimate concerns, but there's another side to the story.

Here are the key factors to consider if you don't have the ability to put down 20%:

- If a lender qualifies you for a loan for the house you want AND you're confident you can cover the monthly mortgage payment based on your current income, seriously consider proceeding even without a 20% down payment.
- If it takes more than six months to save or accumulate a 20% down payment, consider buying with less than 20% down.
- If you wait for that 20% down payment, two principal factors can knock you out of the market for the home you're considering and the loan for which you now qualify.
  - ◊ The first is that interest rates can increase. Increased interest rates can result in higher monthly payments than you have the capability to cover and you'll have to pass on the house you wanted.
  - ◊ The second factor is that home prices rise—much faster than you might imagine—and you can price yourself out of the market for the type of house and area where you can currently buy. Home values can rise much faster than you can save money to put down

that 20%, so if you wait and don't buy now, you may lose the equity you'd be building as a homeowner. Remember, if you continue to pay rent, you're buying real estate for someone else, not investing in your own real estate, and not building up equity.

Recall the story from earlier in the book, when Brother A bought a new home right away with 5% down, and Brother B waited five years until he could save to put down 20%. The infographic below says it all regarding the downside of waiting to buy.

BROTHER A & BROTHER B

CASH
Cost of Waiting To Buy — **$28,643**

Brother A bought right away with 5% down vs. waiting five years and put $28,643 more in his pocket than his brother.

EQUITY
Cost of Waiting To Buy — **$110,565**

Brother A bought right away vs. waiting five years and wound up with $110,565 more equity than his brother.

TOTAL CASH & EQUITY
Cost of Waiting To Buy — **$139,208**

Brother A bought right away and was in much better financial shape—up $139,208—than his brother after five years.

GIFT MONEY

Because one of the biggest challenges in purchasing a home is coming up with the down payment, conventional and FHA lenders allow you to use gift funds from family members. Conventional and FHA lenders will allow 100% of the required down payment to be gift funds from family members or guardians!

For example, if the home you want to buy is $350,000 and the required down payment is 3%, a gift of $10,500 from a family member will come close to moving you into that home. You also need to factor in closing costs which, in some circumstances, the seller can help you pay. We'll discuss later in the book.

The lender requires a gift letter from the donor that lists the following:

- Names and their familial relationship, or the name of the guardian giving the gift
- Amount of the gift
- Verification that the gift does not have to be paid back
- Donor bank name and last four digits of the bank account number
- Donor signatures

Before you receive any gift funds, speak with your mortgage professional about the guidelines and how you should have the money transferred. All funds, especially FHA financing, require supporting documentation such as bank statements showing the donor's ability to give you the gift and a paper trail showing the source of the funds. The amount stated in the gift letter must also match the funds deposited into your account or wired to the title company.

Make sure that any family members giving you the gift understand, from the start of the process, that they must provide a gift letter and, depending on the type of loan or lender, may be required to open up bank records that show the source of the funds. I recently had clients who received a gift of $20,000 from their parents. The father had no problem signing and sending the gift letter but was adamant about not providing the lender with his bank statement showing the source of the funds. My advice is that you check with your lender regarding alternative strategies they'll consider if your family member does not want to provide a bank statement.

APPROACHING FAMILY MEMBERS FOR A GIFT

Many people ask how to go about getting gift money from family members. Here are the key points:

- Know exactly how much money you have to come up with, including the down payment and closing costs.
- Identify how much money you can save on your own.
- Know what your monthly payments will be and what you are capable of paying. There's no point bringing family members into the picture until you've covered all your other bases.
- Provide your family members with a written overview of exactly how much you require, why you need that amount, and what they must do to give a gift that the lender will accept. Do this as part of the pre-approval process.

- Allow family members time so they don't feel rushed, both because they'll be more likely to make the gift and because it will reduce any potential hard feelings after the fact.
- Offer your family members the chance to sit down with your mortgage professional and ask questions they have about the process and why their gift is necessary.

You want the gift of down payment funds from your family to be a positive, affirming experience for all involved; one that strengthens rather than stresses the most important relationships in your life.

CHAPTER 7

CAPABILITY—THE THIRD "C"

Before digging more deeply into the final C, your capability, let's briefly recap the first two C's of home financing. The first C is your credit history as reflected by your credit score, which gives us a good idea of the interest rate you'll receive and the types of loans—both conventional and FHA—for which you'll qualify.

The second C, collateral, is the kind of property, like a single-family residence or condo, that you're buying. We discussed how lenders will assess your collateral using their LTV formula; the size of the down payment you can pay; and how those factors, combined with your credit score, determine the loan terms they will offer you.

Capability is the third C, the keystone of the home financing arch, and the piece that holds everything together. In the home financing world, capability focuses on the size of a monthly mortgage payment you can afford, based on your monthly income and balanced against other monthly debt-related payments you must make. Some finance professionals insist that your monthly mortgage payment shouldn't exceed 25% of your monthly gross income, while others recommend that a much higher percent of your gross income go to your mortgage to optimize tax deductibility benefits.

Because finance professionals sometimes give contradictory recommendations, you need to carefully assess the size of the monthly mortgage payment that feels appropriate for you. The last thing you need is to take the largest loan a lender qualifies you for and then discover that making the mortgage payments causes you enormous stress or you no longer have funds for commitments that matter to you and your family.

- In some geographic areas, higher home prices may require higher mortgage payments than you would pay where prices are lower. In some places, you can get a nice home for $150,000, whereas in Southern California, where I work, the least expensive houses start at $400,000 to $500,000. These higher prices mean that potential homeowners, especially first-time buyers, will need a larger mortgage with a monthly payment that's a higher percentage of their gross income.

Your personal values and preferences may also influence the size of the mortgage and monthly mortgage payment that feels right for you. Some clients want plenty of expendable income after meeting their mortgage commitments, while others are happy to put a larger percentage of their income into their home because it's central to their daily lives. One couple took on a bigger mortgage because it was essential they have a pool to enjoy as a family AND so their home would be an attractive place for their kids and their friends to hang out. On the other hand, I've had clients who were passionate about traveling, and that meant buying a smaller property with lower payments and having more expendable income. So while there are formal indicators of your capability to manage a mortgage, *your* definition of your capability is at least as important, especially when you factor in what you value.

DEBT-TO-INCOME RATIO

In a nutshell, the debt-to-income ratio is how lenders determine your capability to manage a monthly mortgage payment. Three main factors determine your debt-to-income ratio:

- Your total gross income before taxes are deducted.
- Your current total monthly debt payments. There are specific types of debt that lenders include in this figure that we'll look at shortly.
- The estimated monthly payment you'll make to cover your mortgage payment. This payment includes the principal, interest, property taxes, and homeowners insurance—also referred to as PITI. Where applicable, the PITI can include mortgage insurance and HOA fees.

According to the industry standard for the debt-to-income ratio, your combined monthly debt and mortgage payments should use no more than 43% of your gross monthly income or 43 cents of every gross dollar you earn.

Under current guidelines, conventional loans may permit a debt-to-income ratio of up to 49.9%. FHA will allow a ratio up to 56.9%. This can be helpful for people with lower incomes or for self-employed borrowers who have income that is difficult for the lender to verify.

To get the higher ratio, you may need something to offset the risk to the lender, like a good credit score, a larger down payment, or cash reserves.

For those interested in math formulas, see the debt-to-income infographic on the next page.

DEBT TO INCOME RATIO	
$\dfrac{\text{PITI \& OTHER DEBT}}{\text{GROSS INCOME}} =$	DEBT TO INCOME RATIO

Using this method, if your gross income is $5,000 per month, and your combined debt and new mortgage payments are $2,000 a month, divide $2,000 by $5,000, and you get a debt-to-income ratio of 40%, as the chart below indicates.

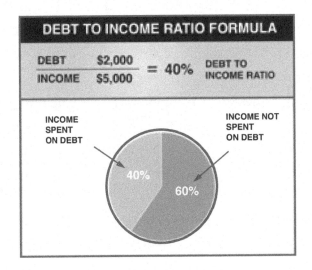

THE CASE OF ERIC

Let's look at how the debt-to-income process worked when a client of mine named Eric was seeking a mortgage. To get rolling, we gathered all of Eric's key financial information and ran his application through an automated underwriting engine developed by Fannie Mae. It tells us whether Eric's loan request will be *credit approved*. Based on Eric's ability to meet conditions of the approval, such as providing paystubs and tax returns, a loan was approved for $297,000.

Before continuing with Eric's story, let's look at what happens when a request for financing is declined by the lender after it's been conditionally approved by the underwriting engine. My experience is that about 30% of applicants who are initially turned down for a loan by one lender can get another lender to approve a loan in thirty days or less. And an additional 40% of those initially declined can get loan approval within six to twelve months.

So don't despair if the underwriting engine for Fannie Mae or Freddie Mac approves your loan but the lender then declines. Being rejected does happen, but you'll still have a good chance of getting approved for a loan by another lender, hopefully sooner rather than later.

A principal reason that certain lenders decline a loan application that the underwriting engine conditionally approved is they impose *lender overlays*. The overlays are additional conditions above those the approval engine requires which can lower a lender's risk of making loans that may default. One example of an overlay is where the underwriting engine may approve a debt-to-income ratio of 48%, but the lender may have an overlay not to exceed 43%.

Another possibility is the underwriting engine asks for one year of tax returns, but a lender overlay insists on two years. This two-year requirement can be problematic for a self-employed individual who experiences fluctuations in annual income from one year to the next.

The lender overlay list can go on forever. The lesson is that not all lenders are created equal. You need a mortgage professional who has relationships with multiple lending sources and will put in the time and effort to make owning a home a reality for you. A mortgage professional willing to go the extra mile can save you an enormous amount of time and frustration, and may well determine whether you achieve your dream of owning a home.

Returning to Eric's loan request, I was excited that Eric was approved for a $297,000 loan but thought he could get better terms if we improved his financials in a couple of places. We rolled up our sleeves and created a strategy to get him a better deal.

Here was Eric's financial profile at the beginning of our process:

- Gross income of $74,000 a year or $6,167 a month
- Credit score of 657, based on high credit card balances and collection accounts
- Savings of 33,000 available for the down payment
- Student loan payment of $198 a month
- Other debt, including an auto loan and credit cards, of $22,500, with monthly payments of $650

To get better loan terms, Eric had three main options:

- Pay down his debt
- Take actions to increase his credit score, which would result in lowering both his interest rate and mortgage insurance
- Increase the down payment. This wasn't an option for Eric because the limited gift funds that he received from his parents were set aside for the closing costs.

Eric pursued the first two options. First, I advised Eric to reduce his down payment to 5%, or $16,500. This move freed up the other $16,500 he'd saved. We used a chunk of that to reduce his other debts. He paid down his $6,000 car loan to where there were only ten months of payments left. Most lenders don't count ten months or less of installment payments as debt, so this was a smart strategy. He paid off $12,000 in credit card debt, reducing his monthly *other debt* payments from $848 to $333 a month. This included his student loan payment of $198 a month. I helped Eric delete two small collection accounts by paying off those balances.

We did a rapid rescore and, to our delight, we qualified him for a much better deal. Take a look at the *before* and *after* figures on the next page, especially the loan amount, interest rate, and the dramatic reduction in his total monthly payments, including his mortgage payments!

ERIC'S FINANCIAL SITUATION
Before and After Debt Reduction Strategy

Home Purchase Price $330,000	Income $74,000	Savings $33,000
	BEFORE	**AFTER**
Down Payment	10%—$33,000 All savings	5%—$16,500 Half of savings
Credit Card Debt	$16,500	$4,500 Reduced by $12,000 from savings
Other Monthly Debt Includes Credit Card, Auto & Student Loans	$848	$333 Credit cards balance reduced. Auto paid down to ten months.
Debt to Income Ratio	49%	39% Lower due to lower debt
Credit Score	657	727 Increase due to reduced debt and collection accounts
Loan Amount	$297,000	$313,500 Increase due to lower down payment
Interest Rate	4.500%	3.875% Lower due to higher credit score
Monthly Home Payments Mortgage, MI, Property Tax, Insurance	$2,181 +	$2,045 +
Monthly Debt & Student Loan Payments	$848	$333
Total Monthly Payments	$3,029	$2,378

As you can see, the combination of paying off debt and increasing Eric's credit score gave him the best of both worlds:

- Eric's debt-to-income ratio dropped from 49% to 39%.
- His credit score increased from 657 to 727 making a sizable decrease in the interest rate and the cost of mortgage insurance.

- For qualifying purposes, his total monthly payments dropped a whopping $651.00!

Improving credit and restructuring a loan not only allows home buyers to decrease their mortgage payment and substantially reduce their total monthly debt payments, but it can also enable them to increase the amount of the home purchase price if the home they want is in a higher price range. For example, with conventional financing and a 5% down payment, the purchase price for Eric could rise from $330,000 to $430,000! Furthermore, Eric's improved credit score would allow him to use lender paid mortgage insurance, resulting in an increased purchase price of up to $450,000. And, if he went with FHA financing, he would qualify for a purchase price of up to $500,000!

The different variations and options when reducing debt and increasing one's credit score can be endless, and a competent mortgage professional who can walk you through the pros and cons of various scenarios is invaluable.

To see how dramatically a person's amount of debt can impact the type and size of loan they're eligible for, look at the infographic on the next page. It shows that if your monthly debt payments, which includes your mortgage payment, rise from around $2,700 a month to almost $4,000 a month, the loan you qualify for drops from $450,000 to under $250,000. That's a pretty dramatic change!

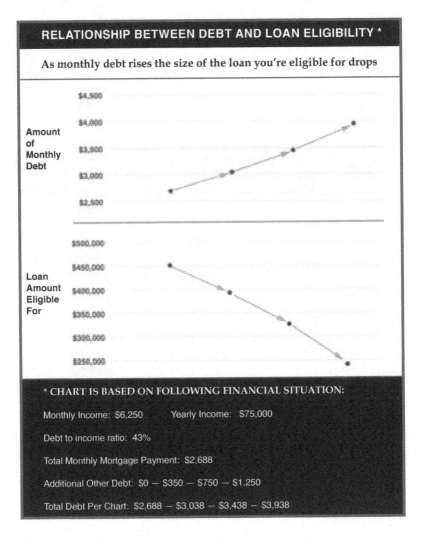

RELATIONSHIP BETWEEN DEBT AND LOAN ELIGIBILITY *

As monthly debt rises the size of the loan you're eligible for drops

* CHART IS BASED ON FOLLOWING FINANCIAL SITUATION:

Monthly Income: $6,250   Yearly Income: $75,000

Debt to income ratio: 43%

Total Monthly Mortgage Payment: $2,688

Additional Other Debt: $0 — $350 — $750 — $1,250

Total Debt Per Chart: $2,688 — $3,038 — $3,438 — $3,938

NOT ALL DEBT IS CREATED EQUAL

Lenders have a precise definition of *debts* when calculating your debt-to-income ratio. Here's a quick breakdown of the debt they include and exclude.

CALCULATING YOUR DEBT TO INCOME RATIO What debt is included in bank calculations?	
INCLUDED	**NOT INCLUDED**
Credit cards	Utilities bills
Installment debt*	Auto insurance
Real estate loans	Church contributions
Other debts	Charitable donations
Mortgage Principal and Interest	Cable or satellite TV bills
Other financing	Cell phone bill
Real estate taxes	Life, disability, dental, and health insurance
Insurance	Savings; 401k; IRA
HOA fees	Childcare
Mortgage insurance	
Spousal & Child Support	
* auto loans, student loans, boat and recreational loans	

As the graphic indicates, lenders only take into consideration specific types of debt payments and don't count all the other expenses you regularly incur. If you have commitments such as charitable gifts to your church or a large monthly childcare or private school payment, you may have less disposable money than the bank thinks you do. When determining what you're capable of paying, factor in all the other monthly costs you have, in addition to the debts your lender lists.

Always remember, capability is not how big of a mortgage you are capable of qualifying for, but how capable you are of comfortably managing and paying for the mortgage you receive.

TAX CUTS & JOBS ACT OF 2017 AND THE MORTGAGE INTEREST DEDUCTION

For many people, there are numerous benefits of homeownership that are more significant than reducing their income taxes. That said, I want you to be aware of how the 2017 tax code affects homeowner-related tax benefits. Here are the three main changes in the tax code that affect homebuyers:

- Increasing the standard deduction for single filers from $6,350 to $12,000, and for joint filers from $12,700 to $24,000.

    ◊ The previous federal tax code favored individuals owning real property, with a key benefit being deducting the interest portion of their mortgage payment. Let's say you were a single filer who earned $75,000 a year, got a $400,000 loan at a 4.5% interest rate, and paid total interest of $18,000 annually. The old mortgage interest deduction would decrease your tax liability by $18,000, to what you'd pay if you made just $57,000 a year.

    ◊ Under the old guidelines, the standard deduction the IRS offered all single filers was $6,350. So you could either take the standard $6,350 deduction or deduct your $18,000 in mortgage interest. You'd take the

$18,000 because that's an extra $11,650 on which you don't have to pay taxes.

◊ Fast-forward to the 2017 tax law. The IRS now gives all single filers a $12,000 standard deduction. You'd be wise to still go with the $18,000 mortgage interest deduction because that includes an extra $6,000 you don't pay taxes on, even if it's not as big of a benefit as before.

- Reduced mortgage interest deduction limit from $1,000,000 to $750,000

  ◊ Borrowers can now deduct interest on mortgage amounts up to $750,000, down from a limit of $1,000,000. If your mortgage is over $750,000, you can still deduct the interest you're paying on the first $750,000 of your total mortgage.

- Limit of $10,000 on combined property tax and state tax deductions.

  ◊ You can now only deduct up to $10,000 in combined property tax and state income taxes. Previously, this deduction amount had been unlimited.

Among the additional variables to factor in when determining how the new tax law affects you personally as a homebuyer are your total income and your ability to itemize other deductible expenses. There are so many changes in the 2017 tax code that I strongly recommend that all homebuyers consult with a CPA to best understand the tax benefits of homeownership for their unique situation.

To give you one concrete example of the impact of the new tax law, let's look at its effect on our Brother A and Brother B from earlier in the book.

THE MORTGAGE INTEREST DEDUCTION—BROTHER A AND BROTHER B

Brother A used his inheritance to buy a home with 5% down while Brother B waited for five years until he'd saved enough to put down 20%. Because Brother B did not buy a home, he had no mortgage interest expense for those five years. Under the new tax law, Brother B can take the standard deduction of $12,000, a significant increase from the previous standard deduction of $6,350.

Brother A had a mortgage and paid interest which was deductible. Even in the new 2017 tax scenario, he still comes out ahead, benefiting from a whopping $25,042 tax deductions, as follows:

- Mortgage interest expense: $15,914
- Real estate taxes: $4,688
- Charity $1,500
- State taxes: $2,940

Since Brother A's mortgage interest expense is so much greater than the standard deduction, he can itemize expenses, reducing his taxable income from $75,000 to $49,958. That's still a better position than Brother B, whose taxable income only drops from $75,000 to $63,000. While the homeowner related tax benefit is not as large as in the previous tax law, it can still be significant.

This example shows that for some people, a significant benefit of using part of their housing expense as a deduction is it allows them to itemize various other costs not related to their housing expense—expenses that, in most cases, they could not deduct if they didn't own a home. For instance, Brother A gave a donation of

$1,500 which is now fully deductible based on his ability to itemize his deductions.

The tax benefits of being a homebuyer can vary greatly depending on personal circumstances, so be sure to seek out the advice of a qualified tax professional in assessing how it impacts your situation. And remember, there are still many benefits to owning a home that outweigh any tax benefits that come your way.

A LAST WORD ON THE THREE "C'S"

We've now covered the three pieces in your home financing arch: Credit, Collateral, and Capability. With this new knowledge, you have an inside track on how lenders will look at your personal loan application.

You now have a better idea of how to manage and repair your credit, a better understanding of the factors involved in determining the size of a down payment and qualifying for a loan, and the ability to understand the size of loan you can afford. This knowledge is the first big chunk of information you need to create your personal strategy for finding and buying a home.

Take a deep breath and congratulate yourself. Now get ready to learn how to find the mortgage that best suits your requirements and how to build your personal home buying dream team.

PART 3

A GREAT MORTGAGE IS
WAITING FOR YOU

CHAPTER 8

HOW MORTGAGES WORK

My goal is to help you get the home financing option with the best possible terms and the best fit for your particular needs and aspirations. In this chapter we explore key mortgage principles such as amortization, explain how to make amortization work to your benefit, and give you the keys to finding and securing the best interest rate.

To get started, let's take a very quick trip back in time to what the home financing market looked like before the big financial crisis that started in 2007. It will help explain why it might seem that there are an awful lot of hoops you need to jump through to get financing.

MORTGAGES BEFORE AND AFTER THE FINANCIAL CRASH ERA

The financial crisis that began in 2007 resulted in thousands of people losing their jobs and the loss of billions of dollars in stock funds, pensions, and retirement funds. Many regular folks saw their life savings vaporized, while others lost their entire retirement nest egg.

Before the mortgage crisis, it seemed like mortgages simply appeared at your command. All you had to do was apply and, "Poof!" the loan documents were there, ready for you to sign. Even with a low credit score, you could get a subprime loan based on the following guidelines:

- 100% financing options—no down payment.
- No verification of whether you had money for the down payment.
- No verifying the source of your down payment.
- No verification of income—only if you had a job.
- No income stated on the application (for some loans)!
- No independent certification of property value.

In other words, if you could fog a mirror with your breath, you could get a loan! The following illustration says it all.

"Let's see, no current job, no job history, dicey credit report, congratulations Ed, you're approved!"

By the end of 2007, the home financing pendulum swung 180 degrees, and the great mortgage credit squeeze kicked in. Here is what was happening when someone applied for a loan in my local area of Southern California. In January 2007, if I received a mortgage approval for one of my clients, there would be five to eight conditions to be satisfied before the lender would fund the loan. Zoom forward twelve months to January 2008. Now a buyer comes to me with a high credit score and stable income—clearly a low risk—and lenders are demanding that thirty to forty conditions be satisfied before they fund a loan! That's a four- to eight-fold increase in conditions a borrower has to satisfy!

As a result of the mortgage meltdown, lenders now ask for much more documentation. I don't like all of the new conditions, but no one wants to see a repeat of thousands of people losing their life savings, their homes, and their livelihoods.

TWO KEY LESSONS LEARNED

If you are buying a new home today, here are two key lessons from the mortgage meltdown:

- Carefully consider your ability to pay the mortgage you're applying for. Don't go for the largest mortgage you can get. Get the mortgage you can manage best.
- Don't count on factors beyond your control, like increased home values or reduced refinancing interest rates, to save you if you're struggling with mortgage payments.

While lenders are now often asking for more information and verification than seems necessary, the situation is better than it was. That's good for the stability of our entire economic system and the housing market, and it makes your new home investment far more secure over the long term.

UNDERSTANDING MORTGAGES = UNDERSTANDING AMORTIZATION

Amortization is a schedule of payments set up by lenders that requires you to pay scheduled monthly payments, so you pay off your mortgage by the end of a given period. These payments include an amount that will pay down the principal you owe and another amount that pays down the interest. Seems innocuous enough, right?

Here's the deal. Lenders have designed amortization, so they get paid the majority of their interest in the early years of the loan. For example, if you have a $260,000 mortgage at a rate of 4.375%, in the first ten years you'll pay almost $120,000 in interest while paying down only $50,000 of your principal! Seriously. This equation slowly reverses as you continue paying on your loan until the bulk of each payment finally goes to paying down the principal. The infographic on the next page is a good illustration of how amortization works.

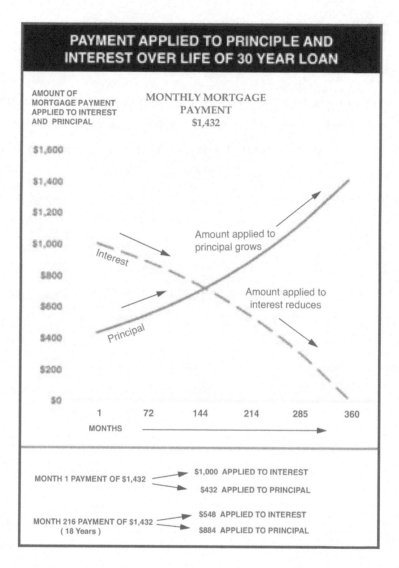

As you can see, when making the first mortgage payment of $1,432, about $1,000 goes to interest and $432 pays down the principal. By about month one hundred forty-four, or twelve years into paying the mortgage, equal amounts of around $716 go to interest and are allocated to reducing the principal. By your final payment, virtually all of the $1,432 payment is paying off the principal. I hope you can see how it would be to your advantage if more of your payment were going to paying down the principal sooner because that also reduces the amount of interest you wind up paying. There are some terrific strategies for doing just that, which we'll get to shortly.

Remarkably, some financial professionals will encourage you to pay as much as possible in interest on your mortgage because interest payments may be tax deductible. I don't believe that this is a wise strategy. I'm totally on board with using tax deductibility for income tax purposes, but I'm not on board with paying any more interest than necessary, especially with the new 2017 tax reform law where the benefits of tax deductibility have been reduced.

USE AMORTIZATION TO YOUR BENEFIT

I want to put you, not the lender, in the driver's seat, so let me introduce you to a process called *accelerating your mortgage*. This process is the most powerful strategy out there to make amortization work for you. Here is how it works.

Let's say you are getting a $300,000 mortgage. The lender will give you a loan schedule that not only shows you the amount of your monthly payment but indicates how much of each payment goes to pay the principal and how much goes to pay interest. Take a look at the amortization schedule on the next page.

SAMPLE AMORTIZATION SCHEDULE

30 YR Fixed Mortgage for $300,000   Interest Rate: 4.375%

Amortization Schedule For Year One

Payment No.	Start Balance	Interest	Principal	Payment Amount	Remaining Balance
1	$300,000	$1,094	$404	$1,498	$299,596
2	$299,596	$1,092	$406	$1,498	$299,190
3	$299,190	$1,091	$407	$1,498	$298,783
4	$298,783	$1,089	$409	$1,498	$298,375
5	$298,375	$1,088	$410	$1,498	$297,965
6	$297,965	$1,086	$412	$1,498	$297,553
7	$297,553	$1,085	$413	$1,498	$297,140
8	$297,140	$1,083	$415	$1,498	$296,726
9	$296,726	$1,082	$416	$1,498	$296,310
10	$296,310	$1,080	$418	$1,498	$295,892
11	$295,892	$1,079	$419	$1,498	$295,473
12	$295,473	$1,077	$421	$1,498	$295,052

The above schedule shows that just $404 goes to pay down the principal in the first payment. To accelerate your mortgage, you want to pay the $406 due on the principal in Payment 2 when you make Payment 1. So your first total payment will be $1,498+$406.

Consequently, in the first month, you're making your first principal payment AND your second principal payment—which you'd have to make eventually—but you're now making it a month sooner. This second payment wipes out all of the interest expense—$1,092—that you would have owed on the second payment. Seriously. You can see how this works in the following infographic.

ACCELERATING YOUR MORTGAGE

30 YR Fixed Mortgage of $300,000   Interest Rate: 4%

① Prepay 2nd month principal of $406

② Wipe out 2nd month interest of $999

Month	Payment	Principal	Pre-Paid Principal	Interest	Payment + Pre-paid Principal	Interest Saved
1	$1,498	$404	$406	$1,094	$1,904	
2	$1,498	$406		$1,092		$1,092
2	$1,498	$407	$409	$1,091	$1,907	
3	$1,498	$409		$1,089		$1,089
3	$1,498	$410	$412	$1,088	$1,910	
4	$1,498	$412		$1,086		$1,086
4	$1,498	$413	$415	$1,085	$1,913	
5	$1,498	$415		$1,083		$1,083
5	$1,498	$416	$418	$1,082	$1,916	
6	$1,498	$418		$1,080		$1,080
6	$1,498	$419	$421	$1,079	$1,919	
7	$1,498	$421		$1,077		$1,077
7	$1,498	$422	$424	$1,076	$1,922	
8	$1,498	$424		$1,074		$1,074
8	$1,498	$425	$427	$1,073	$1,925	
9	$1,498	$427		$1,071		$1,071
9	$1,498	$428	$430	$1,070	$1,928	
10	$1,498	$430		$1,068		$1,068
10	$1,498	$431	$433	$1,067	$1,931	
11	$1,498	$433		$1,065		$1,065
11	$1,498	$435	$436	$1,063	$1,934	
12	$1,498	$436		$1,062		$1,062
12	$1,498	$438	$439	$1,060	$1,937	
13	$1,498	$439		$1,059		$1,059

Total Savings In Interest for Year 1 —— $12,906

Total Savings In Interest over Loan Term —— $119,341

The infographic shows the impact of accelerating your mortgage for the first twelve months of your loan term, during which you'll save $12,906 in interest. Over the entire term of the loan, if you consistently accelerate your mortgage, your savings can total $119,341. And remember, you are double paying only your principal payment, in this case $406, and not doubling your entire mortgage payment of $1,498!

Using the double principal payment strategy, you've accelerated the pay down of your mortgage by one month. Most importantly, you've skipped one month of paying interest on a 30-year fixed mortgage. Instead of having three hundred fifty-nine payments left, you have three hundred fifty-eight payments.

When I explain this concept, some of my clients ask, "Why not just get a shorter-term 20-year or 15-year fixed rate loan?" The problem for many people is they may not qualify for the shorter term loan because of the locked in higher payments. With the 30-year fixed loan, you have the flexibility of either making double principal payments every month or, if you can't afford that, just making a few double principal payments a year—which still eliminates significant interest expense. And anytime you eliminate interest that you're paying, a greater portion of your payment is reducing the principal balance of your loan, which can make a sizable difference when selling your home or fully paying off the mortgage.

By making double principal payments, you're collapsing your amortization schedule. If you make a double principal payment every month for the life of a 30-year fixed loan, you'll pay your loan off in fifteen years AND potentially save yourself hundreds of thousands of dollars in interest.

Here's a fundamental part of this strategy: it's far more useful to accelerate your mortgage in the early years because you pay so much more interest in the first half of the loan. Most people think paying double principal means to double your total mortgage payment. NO! This is not the case. It's merely making an extra principal payment.

To get an idea of the impact of accelerating your mortgage on the amount of equity you have in your house, take a look at the following chart. Your equity is the portion of the house's value you own rather than what the bank owns!

ACCELERATING YOUR MORTGAGE INCREASES EQUITY
30 YR Fixed Mortgage for $300,000 Interest Rate: 4.375%

Impact of Paying Double Principal on Your Equity

Standard Payments		Pay Double Principle	
	Equity		**Equity**
Year 1	$4,948	Year 1	$10,116
Year 5	$27,048	Year 5	$60,696
Year 10	$60,696	Year 10	$154,629

After 10 years, if you just made standard payments you'd have $60,696 in equity, but if you made double principle payments you'd have $154,629 in equity—a difference of almost $94,000!

The real eye-popping figure in this chart is that by accelerating your mortgage over ten years, you'll increase your home equity by over 250%, from $60,696 to $154,629! That's an increase of nearly $94,000, so if you sell your home after ten years, there's an extra $94,000 going into your pocket. Think about that for a second.

A COMPETITIVE INTEREST RATE IS YOUR GOAL

Something I encourage you NOT to do on your own is to spend days or weeks shopping for the elusive "lowest interest rate on the planet." Clients show up at my office exhausted after trying to shop and compare lenders' rates with complicated spreadsheets they've created. As a general rule, the rates for most lenders, especially the 30-year fixed rate mortgages backed by Fannie and Freddie, are very competitive.

I encourage you not to make getting the lowest interest rate your highest priority. As the title of this section indicates, your goal is to find a *competitive rate*, not the *lowest rate*. There is a big difference between the two. A low rate is exactly that—a low rate, and many times it comes with downsides that make it a real problem during the escrow process. If a lender is giving you such a rate, they're making less money, which means there's a trade-off. Often that involves not providing the necessary resources or training for their team or, even worse, hiring unqualified mortgage professionals. And that can become a big problem for you.

I know of a couple, Bruce and Tammy, who were chasing the lowest interest rate on the planet and ultimately got what seemed to be a terrific deal. However, as often happens in these situations, the lender gave them inadequate information and made promises regarding funding their loan they couldn't keep. In the end, Bruce and Tammy couldn't close escrow on time and paid a significant penalty because they didn't meet their escrow terms. Then their situation went from bad to worse when the lender boosted their interest rate after their original rate lock expired.

I see this all the time with clients who come to me after dealing with these kinds of lenders. We have to start over, pull their credit report again, and sometimes discover that their credit score has dropped, meaning they now have to take a higher interest rate to get a loan. Remember, lenders who offer the lowest rates often provide minimal support and service, so there's an increased risk the deal can blow up.

Competitive interest rates can often be the same or very close to a rock-bottom interest rate while offering many more advantages: the biggest being better service, more safeguards, and more professional interactions. Competitive rates are the ones that mortgage professionals and lenders can actually deliver in the required time frame while still giving you an excellent deal.

I've been in the home financing business for over three decades. Interest rates are funny things; they go up, and they go down. When looking for home financing, the key is finding a qualified mortgage professional you can trust to secure you a competitive rate. I've built my entire business on the commitment to get my clients highly competitive rates with reputable lenders. The result is satisfied individuals who are so happy with their loans that ten years later they ask for my help on refinancing their loan or securing a loan for their new home.

The bottom line is if you choose to shop for that absolute lowest rate, the process may cost more than you think. It may cost you not only thousands of dollars; it may cost your sanity!

WHAT'S THE REAL RATE TO SHOOT FOR?

The interest rate you're most likely to get will not be the one advertised on your TV or radio! The rates rarely reflect the actual rates most people receive or don't even track regular daily interest rate fluctuations.

You only get a real idea of a competitive rate on a given property after a mortgage professional knows the following:

- Your credit score(s)
- Type of loan—FHA or conventional
- Type of property you're buying
- Target loan amount
- Target loan product—30-year fixed versus a 5-year ARM or other type of loan. An ARM is an Adjustable Rate Mortgage.

From a lender's perspective, all interest rates are computed using risk-based pricing. This is calculated based on your credit score and the amount of your down payment. There's no such thing as one rate fits all, even with FHA or VA loans. In most cases, the low advertised rates are based on low LTVs and credit scores of 740.

If you want to get a feel for the rates and terms you qualify for, call a mortgage professional, give them your credit score, debt payment information, gross income, the type of property you want, and what you can afford for a down payment. If you don't have your credit score, ask them to use a hypothetical score or give them an estimate of what you think your score is and plug that into the equation. With all the above information, a mortgage professional can quickly give you an idea of the interest rate, the amount of the loan, the types of loans, and the loan terms for which you'll most likely qualify.

If you don't already have your credit score, do not, under any circumstances, let a mortgage professional pull your credit until you're sure that's the person with whom you want to work. It's vital that you don't have multiple mortgage professionals or lenders pulling your credit report while you are shopping for a loan because that can negatively impact your credit score.

CHAPTER 9

YOU HAVE LOTS OF MORTGAGE OPTIONS

By the time you finish this chapter, you'll understand the main mortgage product options currently available, have a much better sense of the type of mortgage that works best for you, and have the knowledge needed to cut through the mortgage marketing hype you encounter on a daily basis.

But Honey, the bank said we could swing it on a 50 year mortgage.

Let's start by looking at a fundamental concept in the mortgage business called the *time value of money* and how it impacts the types of mortgages currently available.

THE TIME VALUE OF MONEY

When talking about mortgages, a key industry principle is the *time value of money*. The principle of the time value of money is that *the shorter the loan term, the lower the rate*. A big concern for lenders and investors is the opportunity cost of tying up money in a long-term home loan to you for 30 years. By opportunity cost, I mean they're looking at your loan in the context of other, potentially more lucrative investment opportunities where they can get higher returns.

Here is how their thinking goes. If I lend you $260,000 for thirty years, I won't have that $260,000 to invest in anything else for a long time. Ten years into the loan term, I have an opportunity to invest in a hot new company called Microsoft. It's just gone public, and over the next ten years, I could see a ten to twenty-fold return on my investment, whereas the return I'd see on lending you $260,000 at 5% interest over 30 years is a fraction of that. In this example, the opportunity cost of not investing $260,000 in Microsoft stock is very high.

But if I'd loaned you the money for just ten years, maybe I'd have the money back in time to invest in Microsoft. Because lenders want the flexibility to pursue new investment opportunities, they'll charge you higher interest for loan terms they have to live with for thirty years rather than a shorter interval. That's why the lowest interest rates are on shorter term or adjustable rate mortgages. So that's the principle of the time value of money.

FIXED RATE MORTGAGES

The most popular form of home financing is the traditional fixed rate loan. With conventional financing guidelines, you can get a loan with a fixed term between 10 and 30 years, with the most common being a 30-year term. These loans are fully amortized to pay off exactly within the designated period. The interest rate is fixed for the entire term of the loan, so the shorter the term, the higher the payment. You can see below how monthly payments go up from $1,498 to $3,020 as the loan term drops from 30 years to 10 years.

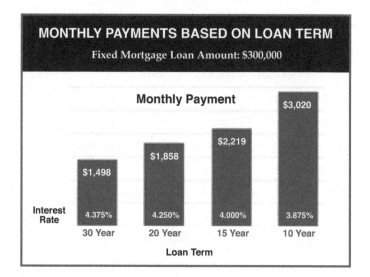

If you want to lower the total amount of interest you pay and have a fixed rate loan, consider a shorter term. While your monthly payments will be higher, a larger percentage of your payment will pay down the principal rather than interest. The next infographic provides a good example of this approach.

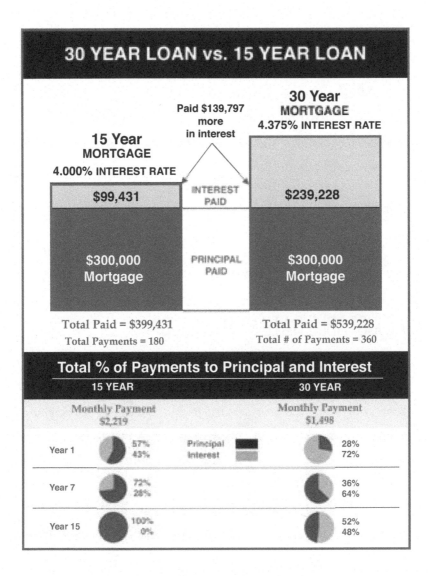

You can see the impact of the 15-year term versus 30 years. On a $300,000 loan, you pay $139,797 less in interest with a 15-year term. That's reduction of almost 60%!

FIXED TERM LOANS—THE GOOD

A couple of further thoughts on the good and the bad of a fixed rate loan. Nothing can replace the security of a fixed rate loan. There is no payment variation, so you know what you pay each month as long as you have the loan. Most lenders like these loans because they have the lowest default rates.

FIXED TERM LOANS—THE BAD

If you plan to be in your new home for only four or five years, you'll pay a higher rate for a long-term fixed loan than you need.

ADJUSTABLE RATE MORTGAGES

Returning to the principle of the time value of money, the longer the term of a loan, the higher the interest rate. If you're not planning to keep your home for an extended period, like thirty years, you don't want to pay the higher rate for a long-term loan. On the other hand, if you reduce the length of a loan, your monthly mortgage payments will be higher—often a lot higher. For example, the monthly payment for a 30-year fixed mortgage of $300,000 at 4.375% is $1,498, but if you reduce the term to 5 years, the monthly payment jumps to $5,576.

Lenders addressed this problem of enormous payments by creating an adjustable rate mortgage, a *blended mortgage* that's amortized over 30 years. It has an introductory period—usually between five to ten years—when they charge you a lower interest rate. Then there's the remaining term of the loan where you'll most likely pay a higher rate based on factors we'll explain.

If you get an ARM and sell your house or refinance the loan before the end of the introductory period, you likely walk away paying a lot less in interest than with a 30-year fixed. The catch is that after the introductory term, your ARM's interest rate is tied to an index that may cause your interest rate and mortgage payments to fluctuate from year to year and, in some cases, jump significantly.

Here is a sample of the various ARMs available in today's marketplace, with their corresponding interest rates and payments. We are using a loan amount of $300,000. As you can see, the shorter the initial term, the lower the interest rate. For example, the introductory term of five years has an initial interest rate of 3.750%, while longer terms have higher initial interest rates.

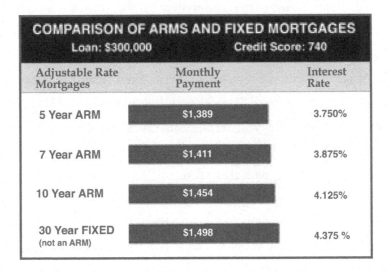

| COMPARISON OF ARMS AND FIXED MORTGAGES | | |
Loan: $300,000		Credit Score: 740
Adjustable Rate Mortgages	Monthly Payment	Interest Rate
5 Year ARM	$1,389	3.750%
7 Year ARM	$1,411	3.875%
10 Year ARM	$1,454	4.125%
30 Year FIXED (not an ARM)	$1,498	4.375 %

Some years ago, I had clients named Joe and Debbie who were moving to our area. Joe was on a fast track in senior management for a large corporation. He was transferring with the understanding that they would be here for five to seven years. That was long enough to warrant buying a home, but not so long that a 30-year fixed mortgage made sense. Joe and Debbie were the perfect candidates for an ARM, due to the lower interest rate they would have before selling the house after five years.

How do you determine if an ARM is a correct move for you? Here are my three main criteria, in order of importance.

First, if you're fairly confident that you'll only keep your home for 5-10 years, consider an ARM. If you hope to settle down in your home for the long haul, then stick with a 15-year or 30-year fixed and proceed to the next chapter. My observation is that, as a general rule, my clients wind up staying in their homes much longer than they originally anticipated. So be careful when choosing your ARM because if you stay past the introductory term there is a good chance your interest rate will rise and your monthly payments will increase.

Second, analyze the difference in the current introductory interest rate for a 5-year ARM and a 30-year fixed. The infographic above shows that for a loan of $300,000, the interest rate on a 5-year ARM is 3.75% vs. 4.375% on a 30-year fixed. That translates into a monthly payment that's $1,389 vs. $1,498, a savings of $109 a month or $6,540 over the 5-year term. Sometimes the disparity between a 5-year ARM and a 30-year fixed can be even more dramatic, in which case consider going with the ARM.

Third, find out to what level the reset interest rate is allowed to rise after the introductory rate expires. If the maximum jump is just 1% or 2%, that shouldn't wipe out the savings you realized in the first five years with the lower ARM rate. However, if it can jump 5% after the initial term expires, that may wipe out any savings you'd have seen, plus a lot more.

If you decide an ARM may be for you, here are key issues to be aware of:

- After the introductory period, interest rates are based on independent indices. The primary index that is currently used is the One Year LIBOR, short for London Interbank Overnight Rate.

- Look for the lowest margin. A margin is a percentage that lenders add to the index rate to calculate the interest rate they'll charge you *after* your ARM's introductory period. If the LIBOR is at 3%, and your margin is 2.75%, your interest rate will be 5.75% after the introductory period. Generally speaking, the lower the margin, the lower the rate.

- Look for the lowest *initial reset adjustment*, which is the maximum that your interest rate can increase for your first reset after the introductory period ends. For example, if an ARM has a five-year introductory period with an initial 2% cap and the LIBOR index is at 3%, the new rate after five years can be no more than 5%. Adjustment caps range from 1% for FHA loans to 5% for conventional loans.

- Always know your worst case scenario. Find out what your highest payment can potentially be, both after the introductory period and over the life of the loan.

- I rarely recommend anything shorter than a seven-year introductory period. Look for the longest introductory period balanced against the lowest interest rate.

THE *GOOD*

Some real benefits of an ARM:

- The interest rate for the introductory period of the loan may be significantly lower than with a 30-year fixed mortgage.

- With a lower interest rate, a larger portion of the mortgage payment pays down the principal.

- If you aren't keeping your home for a long time, the typical 30-year fixed mortgage may prove to be a costly security blanket
- Interest rates cycle up and down. A qualified mortgage professional can help you take advantage of refinancing when interest rates cycle downward.

THE *BAD*

ARMs do have potential downside risks:

- After the introductory period, you may have no option but to pay the higher interest reset rate because 1) you no longer have the credit or income to qualify for a new loan; 2) your property value has fallen; 3) you owe too much on the loan and can't refinance.
- The interest rate may be so high after resetting that you can't make the payments, resulting in foreclosure or bankruptcy.
- You chose an ARM, expecting to stay in your home for a limited time, but stay past the loan's introductory period. You must then consider refinancing or decide to potentially live with a higher reset rate.

The worst-case scenario with an ARM is losing your home to foreclosure because you can't make the higher payments after the reset or can't refinance because of bad credit, lower property values, or lower income. That's the single biggest downside of an ARM. With a 30-year fixed rate mortgage, your interest rate may initially be higher, but you have greater security of knowing the amount you'll pay each month for the entire term of the loan.

"OK, I'm going to say you're quite risk averse."

CLOSING COSTS, POINTS, AND FEES

There are two primary categories of closing costs when buying or refinancing your home: *recurring* and *non-recurring*. In previous sections, we've explained the main recurring closing costs, which include charges you pay over the life of your loan like interest, taxes, insurance fees, and HOA dues.

To make sure that consumers aren't hit with closing cost fees they weren't aware of, the U.S. Consumer Financial Protection Bureau, often referred to as the CFPB, has created a collection of closing documents that all lenders must provide to home buyers who are financing the purchase of their new home. It provides a detailed overview of all recurring and non-recurring costs and fees they will charge. A sample is available online at: http://www.consumerfinance.gov/owning-a-home/closing-disclosure/.

For your convenience, here's most of the recurring and non-recurring closing costs. This list is not a substitute for the information provided by the CFPB, which I recommend that you review.

NON-RECURRING FEES

Please note that the list can vary based on where you live:

- Loan Costs:
  - ◊ Origination fee, which is also called Points
  - ◊ Application fee
  - ◊ Processing fee
  - ◊ Underwriting fee
- Other loan costs:
  - ◊ Appraisal fee
  - ◊ Credit report fee
  - ◊ Flood determination fee
  - ◊ Flood monitoring fee
  - ◊ Tax monitoring fee
  - ◊ Tax status research fee
- Pest inspection fees
- Survey fee
- Title: Insurance Binder
- Title: Lender's title insurance
- Title (escrow): Settlement agent fee
- Title: Title search
- Other costs:
  - ◊ Stamp tax
  - ◊ Recording fees
  - ◊ Transfer tax
  - ◊ Deed
  - ◊ HOA Capital contribution
  - ◊ HOA processing fee
  - ◊ Home inspection fee
  - ◊ Home warranty fee
  - ◊ Title: Owner's title insurance

RECURRING FEES

These are often called pre-paids:

- Homeowner's insurance
- Mortgage insurance premium
- Prepaid interest
- Property taxes

Non-recurring closing costs are charges you pay only once. They're all due at or before closing, which is when the loan is finalized, and all the paperwork is completed for you to take possession of your new home. Non-recurring costs break down into three categories:

- *Lender fees* associated with obtaining mortgage financing include everything from the origination fee or points, to underwriting fees and fees for a credit report, flood certification, the appraisal, and other charges we explain later in the book.
- *Upfront Mortgage Insurance FHA/VA fees* only apply when getting FHA or VA financing. These are often financed as part of the loan and, in most cases, won't come out of your pocket.
- *Closing fees* are charges associated with closing the transaction. These include the cost of the closing attorney or escrow fee, title fees for recording the deed, transfer taxes, and stamp taxes.

THE ORIGINATION FEE

Origination fees are often the largest of the lender fees and are known as points. Each point is equal to 1% of the total amount of the mortgage. If you are getting a $250,000 loan, one point is $2,500, and you must pay that amount at closing.

ORIGINATION FEES

$$\$250{,}000 \quad X \quad 1\% \quad = \quad \$2{,}500$$

Loan Amount	Points	Fees

The simplest explanation of the origination fee is that it's prepaid interest on the loan you're getting. So, the larger the origination fee you pay at closing, the lower your interest rate. To give you that lower interest rate, a lender might charge you one to two points. If you don't pay any points when taking out a loan, there's no way you can get the lowest interest rate. It—is—just—not—possible.

Each point you pay reduces your interest rate on a 30-year fixed mortgage by about 1/8 to 1/4 of a percent. For example, one point would drop an interest rate of 4.375% to 4.125%. A major factor in deciding how many points to pay is estimating how long you plan to keep the home you are buying and the loan you're taking out. A reduction of ¼ of a percent in interest can save you a lot of money if you keep your loan for an extended period of time. However, if you plan to sell or refinance within five years, it may not be worth it.

Let's look at the math. A 30-year fixed loan for $250,000 with an interest rate of 4.5% equals a monthly payment of $1,267. But if you pay one point, or $2,500, at closing, your interest rate drops to 4.25%, which reduces your monthly payment to $1,230. That's a savings of $37 a month.

To calculate whether paying the one point is worth it, divide the $2,500 by your monthly savings of $37. That shows that after 68 months or about 5.6 years, you'll see savings that equal the $2,500 you paid for the one point. Every payment you make after that means $37 a month stays in your pocket rather than going into the lender's.

Over another ten years, that adds up to around $4,440 in savings to you. So, paying that one point up front would be a smart investment.

What you pay in points may be tax deductible, so you'll realize additional savings and your break-even point will be shorter than the 5.6 years.

An important factor in weighing whether to pay points is how much money you have available for a down payment and your other closing costs. If you have limited funds and want to optimize your available cash to purchase the property, it may be to your advantage to reduce your down payment and ask for a zero-point loan. More on that shortly.

I recommend that you never pay more than 1.00 to 1.25 points because anything above that doesn't provide much, if any, upside in reduced interest rates. Paying more than that is just lining your lender's pocket with additional money. In a low-interest rate environment, I favor zero point loans because you don't get that much bang for your buck by reducing your interest rate if you pay even 1.00 point.

HOW ZERO COST LOANS WORK

When lenders advertise to get your business, they use two basic hooks, usually in a single ad. One hook is a loan with absolutely no fees! This offer is referred to as a zero cost loan. The other hook is a loan with a rock bottom interest rate. Both of these hooks work exceptionally well in bringing in new customers—and together they're blockbusters.

There is one big problem with the pitch. It never happens that lenders will give you both a loan with no fees AND the lowest interest rate. The only way to get a very low-interest rate is to pay points. Remember, one way or another, lenders will cover their costs and make a profit on a loan—even if they give you a zero cost loan.

The way a zero cost loan works is the lender gives you a credit that pays for all of your fees. The infographic on the next page shows how one can go from getting a lower interest rate by paying closing fees and more points to having a higher interest rate when paying no points and a lender credit that pays your closing fees:

1. To get a lower interest rate, you pay more points.

2. To pay minimal or zero points, you pay a higher interest rate.

3. To pay zero points AND get a lender credit to pay all of your fees, you pay an even higher interest rate. For example, with a 30-year fixed rate loan, your interest rate is 4.375% if you pay one point. The interest rate rises to 4.50% if you want a zero-point loan. To get a zero *cost* loan, the interest rate goes up even more, to 4.750%. As the infographic on the next page shows:

4. To get the lowest interest rate of 4.375%, as shown in the One Point Loan column, you pay a combination of points and fees.

5. If you don't want to pay points but are willing to pay fees, you get the middle-level interest rate of 4.50%.

6. If you don't want to pay either fees or points, you are charged with the highest interest rate of 4.750%, as shown in the Zero Cost Loan Column.

ZERO POINTS AND ZERO COST LOANS

| $300,000 Loan | Lowest Interest Rate & Payments | Highest Interest Rate & Payments | |
	One Point Loan	Zero Points Loan	Zero Cost Loan
Points	1	0	0
Points in Dollars	$3,000	$0	$0
Loan Fees	$3,125	$3,125	$0
Cost of Loan	$6,125	$3,125	$0
Interest Rate	4.375%	4.500%	4.750%
Monthly Payment	$1,498	$1,520	$1,565
Interest Savings Over 30 Years	$24,151	$16,159	$0
Net Upside in Reduced Interest	$18,026	$13,034	$0

Net Savings Over 30 Years

As the saying goes, "there's no free lunch," and that's the case with home financing. As a home buyer, you need to decide which combination of trade-offs work best for your particular situation.

When you hear an advertisement for a free mortgage, is it really free? The answer, regrettably, is no. Why? Because if a lender gives you a mortgage for free, the interest you'll pay on the loan is higher than the current market rate!

WORD TO THE WISE

Home financing is a multi-billion-dollar business, so lenders spend a ton of money advertising their mortgage deals—on the radio, TV, the internet, and in newspapers and magazines. One problem with mortgage advertising is that, while interest rates fluctuate on a daily basis, lenders can only periodically update the information in their commercials. Consequently, the information you get is often out of date. Thus the legal caveat at the end of most advertisements: *Rates are subject to change without notice.*

If you want to do an analysis of the home financing ads you hear, I've created the following guide to sniffing out those that may be fishy. The key is knowing the clues they leave in the fine print.

Let's do a point by point breakdown of a commercial I heard on the radio recently. "Right now we have a loan with an introductory interest rate of 3.75%, a 30-year amortization, an APR of 4.07%, no points, no fees, not one penny added to your principal." And then comes the fine print in the ad: "We guarantee to give you the lowest rates available. Rates and terms subject to change, actual charges may vary, requires a credit score of 740, LTV of 75%…" You get the idea.

Let's break it down:

- Introductory 3.75% interest rate. *Introductory* is code for saying it's an adjustable rate mortgage and your rate will go up.
- 30-year amortization. This sounds like a 30-year fixed mortgage, but it's an adjustable rate mortgage that's only fixed for the first five years.
- APR or annual percentage rate of 4.07%. It's a dead giveaway that something is fishy when the APR is higher than the

advertised interest rate. If this were a 30-year fixed with no fees, the APR would be equal to the introductory interest rate, something we'll explore later.

- Credit score of 740. This high score always gives you excellent rates and terms.

- Loan to Value of 75%. You will have to put down at least 25%.

- Rates and Prices subject to change. The ad has no explanation of what conditions can cause the changes. Rates continually go up and down, and they may only record an advertisement every few weeks, so the terms they're offering may be very different from what they originally recorded.

- Lowest rates and fees—Anytime you hear a *guarantee* for the lowest rates, that's a huge red flag because in most states the law prohibits lenders from even making this claim.

The next time you look at or listen to a home financing ad, pay attention to the buzzwords and red flags listed above, and you won't have too much trouble sniffing out the ads that are heavy on hype and do the old bait and switch.

TAKING YOUR NEXT BIG STEP

Congratulations on working through the ins and outs of mortgage products, learning how to make amortization work for you, and understanding that your goal is getting a competitive interest rate and not a rock bottom rate.

You now possess all the necessary knowledge you need—and that few new home buyers have—to take the all-important next step and create your home buying dream team!

PART 4

FINDING AND BUYING YOUR NEW HOME

CHAPTER 10

THREE KEY STAGES IN BUYING A HOME

You're ready to apply everything that you've learned to find and buy the home of your dreams! Your path to moving into your new home will unfold over the three phases we cover in the next two chapters. Here is what you can expect during the first two phases.

KEY HOME BUYING PHASES

Phase 1: Preparation

1. Find a qualified mortgage professional
2. Receive pre-approval for a loan you qualify for and can afford
3. Review closing costs and down payment requirements
4. Determine amount of funds you need to close on your home
5. Find a real estate professional

Phase 2: Finding Your Home & Making an Offer

1. Work with real estate professional to identify a home
2. Place offer on the home and use letter from your mortgage professional to show you're pre-approved
3. Negotiate the offer
4. Your offer is accepted

Phase 3: Closing on Your Home

We outline this phase in Chapter 11

Once you navigate these first two phases, you reach the final sprint in the home buying process: the escrow or contract phase often referred to as *closing*. The closing process is fairly extensive in itself, so we'll give you an overview of that process after we've covered Phase One and Phase Two.

CREATING YOUR HOME BUYING DREAM TEAM

There may have been a time in the distant past when a person could find and buy a home all on their own, but those days are long gone. Today the home buying process involves endless arcane details, all sorts of financial and legal disclosures, and insider knowledge about the availability of houses and types of financing. That's why I strongly recommend that you think of buying a home as a team effort and make it a primary goal to put together your home buying dream team.

There are at least three key people on your dream team—a real estate professional, a mortgage professional, and you. If you're married or have a partner, they're the fourth key member of the team, as their participation is essential in evaluating your home buying and financing options and making short and long-term decisions.

Later in this chapter, I've dedicated an entire section to finding a first-rate real estate professional, so, for now, let me just say that the realtor you decide to work with is as important as the mortgage professional you select. They bring specialized knowledge that goes beyond knowing what homes are on the market or coming on the market. Based on their experience of tracking home sales in numerous different neighborhoods, they know homes that are a good deal and homes that are overpriced. They know how to put together an offer on a house that rises to the top of the stack and negotiate a final deal with your best interests in mind. With your mortgage professional, they'll successfully guide you through the all-important escrow and closing process.

One thing I can assure you, when you secure the services of an excellent real estate professional and a first-rate mortgage professional, the stress involved in your home buying process will decrease, and the potential for you to find and buy the home of your dreams will increase dramatically!

YOUR MORTGAGE PROFESSIONAL AS A TRUSTED GUIDE

Unless you thrive on unnecessary stress, taking the time to find a qualified mortgage professional can make all the difference if you want to keep your sanity while seeking the financing you need to buy your new home. Qualified mortgage professionals take their job seriously, treat you and your information with respect, and only make promises they can keep. The mortgage application process is complicated. A lot of things can go wrong if you aren't getting first-rate service.

"I'm afraid your loan will be stuck in underwriting
until you've each had a full panic attack."

Getting a mortgage can be an unsettling and emotional experience. Significant parts of your financial profile can be so intertwined with your personal life experiences that it may feel like you're letting a total stranger read your diary. That's why it's vital to find a mortgage professional who you believe has your best interests at heart and who you trust to tell the truth about what to expect throughout the process of getting a loan.

I want to share a story with you. On a flight home from a business trip, I sat next to a pilot who was a captain for a major airline. He flew the largest jets in his company's fleet and was at the top of his profession.

I'd just read an article about how flight technology was so advanced that an airplane could complete an entire trip, including taking off and landing, without the aid of a pilot. I asked my new found pilot friend if technology was a threat to his job. His response both surprised and impressed me. "Pilots are not there to fly the plane. They are there to fix unexpected problems that the computers can't fix."

Even the most experienced home buyer quickly discovers that unexpected challenges always arise as part of the home financing process. While computers and online loan applications can be handy, when the process gets turbulent, you'll be relieved that you partnered with an experienced mortgage professional to help you navigate any stormy skies and find the clearest route forward.

PREPARATION AND REPUTATION ARE EVERYTHING

If you aren't receiving exceptional service, getting a mortgage can be very stressful. The last thing you need is an unqualified mortgage professional driving the process—and potentially driving you—on a wild ride and over the cliff.

Think about getting a mortgage as a three stage process:

1. Preparing the application
2. Getting your loan formally approved
3. Closing the loan

A qualified mortgage professional understands that 75% of the work should focus on preparing your application correctly and in great detail at the beginning of the loan process. This work results in minimal follow-up questions from the loan underwriter approving your mortgage and fewer complications when funding the loan at closing.

When thinking about the mortgage application and approval process, I like to use the analogy of launching a rocket into space, where you use 80% of the fuel during liftoff and the first few minutes of flight, with smooth flying after that. When that doesn't happen, you have a rocket that hardly gets off the ground in the first place or goes off course, runs out of fuel and crashes. Getting a mortgage is not rocket science, however, with the increased regulations and loan underwriting guidelines, sometimes it feels close to it.

An incompetent mortgage professional often starts with a rushed preparation process, then tons of follow-up questions because they poorly completed the application in the first place, and lots of last minute drama at closing.

With a mortgage application, the devil is in the details, and getting the details right in the first place often determines your stress level and whether you get a loan approval. Equally important, if the loan underwriter notices any red flags related to the initial submission of your application, it can become a slippery slope because they begin paying closer attention and looking for other potential issues.

The following infographic shows how a qualified mortgage professional focuses a majority of the work during preparation, with minimal work at the end of the process, whereas the unqualified professional spends minimal time in preparation and significant time scrambling to respond to lender inquiries. For every hour you spend correctly preparing the application in the first place, you'll save countless hours of scrambling down the line. As the saying goes, an ounce of prevention is worth a pound of cure. However, in the mortgage business, an ounce of prevention is worth ten pounds of cure.

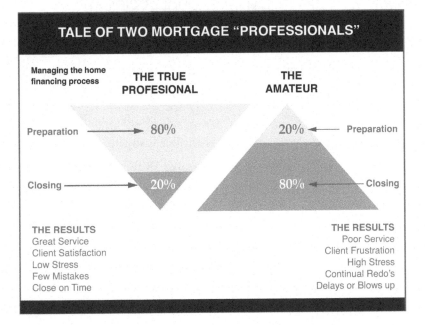

Be aware that the reputation of the person or company who prepares and submits your loan application will, in many cases, either speed up or slow down your approval. Underwriters sometimes select application files that they choose to push to the top of their stack for processing. If they see applications prepared by mortgage professionals they respect and who submit clean and accurate applications, many times they'll process those first. Those applications take less work, require fewer follow-up requests to the loan officer, and can be approved more quickly. In the home financing business, reputation is everything.

TALE OF TWO MORTGAGE "PROFESSIONALS"

I'd like to introduce you to two mortgage professionals, one very qualified, who we will call Attentive Amy, and one truly unqualified, who we'll call Snafu Sam. Let's begin with Attentive Amy.

Attentive Amy is the kind of a highly qualified mortgage professional you want on your team because she's attentive to your needs and pays attention to the details. She's interested in you as a real person with dreams and hopes. She gets right down to business, wanting to understand your situation and your needs. She makes no big promises but makes a commitment to work closely with you to find the best rates and the best loan program and to do this in a way that creates an enjoyable, low-stress experience for you.

Attentive Amy is all over the details. You ask a specific question and get your question answered. You call her office, and she either picks up right away or is back to you within the same day!

She asks for all the documentation up front and places her attention on the preparation stage of the loan. She structures your loan, identifies potential problems, and reviews them with you. You keep thinking, "Wow, she knows what she's doing."

Attentive Amy is willing to go the extra mile, preparing a cover letter to the underwriter explaining why your loan should be approved. At least 80% of her efforts go into completing your initial loan application.

Your loan is approved with few surprises because Attentive Amy had thoroughly organized and carefully prepared the documents before your loan was submitted. You sign the loan documents, your loan is funded and is recorded with minimum effort and drama. The loan documents are ready in time for you to carefully review before you close on your home, giving you plenty of time to ask questions. Most importantly, Attentive Amy has walked you through the estimated closing costs before you go to sign your loan papers, so there are no surprises at the last minute.

Now let's meet Snafu Sam, an *unqualified* mortgage professional if you ever saw one. I want you to get to know him here so that you never, ever, wind up working with him in real life.

Snafu Sam is all about big promises. He can get you any loan you want. "It will be a piece of cake." He makes big promises but isn't too big on the details. "Don't worry about it." "Just need a couple more things." "It's all good." These are Sam's go-to lines.

You can tell right away he's not too organized. He may make mistakes when calculating your income or debt. Or he says he has all the needed information and then quickly calls back and mentions he needs something else. When you call him for something, he never seems to be around and often forgets to return your calls. You ask for specifics; you get vague answers. You show concern; he tells you not to sweat it.

As the loan process moves towards closing, Snafu Sam continues asking for more documentation. You become frustrated and irritated that the process is not as easy as he led you to believe. Every time you speak with Snafu Sam, he assures you he needs just one more piece of documentation. You hear "no problem" a little too often.

"No problem! We'll document the income later."

Before closing, you discover your interest rate is higher than expected or your loan program has changed. But you are locked in. Your worst nightmares are confirmed. Your stress levels shoot through the roof. There is growing tension on your home front. Closing the loan is a monumental effort and comes close to requiring you to cancel your purchase and possibly lose your deposit. Your experience of getting a mortgage makes you wonder if renting for the rest of your life isn't such a bad idea—all because of the incompetence of an unqualified mortgage professional.

While there are many Attentive Amy's in the world of home financing, there are also some Snafu Sam's. I want to make sure you have the information you need to find the right person for your situation. As the first step in that process, let's review the types of mortgage professionals available in today's market.

FINANCIAL INSTITUTIONS AND MORTGAGE PROFESSIONALS

The two most important characteristics of a mortgage professional are: 1) they are honest and can be trusted to look out for your best interests; 2) they know the business inside and out. If they have these two qualities, the prospects of having a smooth transaction are substantially enhanced.

Mortgage professionals come in all shapes and sizes and work for one of three types of financial institutions. The first two we'll look at are a traditional bank and a mortgage bank. These are direct lenders, which means that they fund your loan with their own money.

The first is the traditional bank, formally referred to as a depository financial institution. In this case, the mortgage professional works for the bank that funds your loan from deposits made by individuals and businesses into the bank's accounts.

The second type of financial institution that mortgage professionals work for is a mortgage bank, which gets money to fund your loan from lines of credit it has arranged. A mortgage bank then sells the loans it makes to investors in the secondary market, who then pay back the mortgage bank's line of credit, enabling it to lend more money.

The third type of financial institution is a mortgage brokerage. They don't fund your loan directly from their own funds or lines of credit but perform all other key home financing functions as a mortgage bank or traditional bank. Their specialty is putting you, the borrower, together with the lending source most appropriate for your capabilities and financing needs.

I've worked for each of these types of institutions and currently own a mortgage brokerage. Mortgage professionals working for any of these institutions can provide first-rate service to home buyers seeking financing.

FINDING A QUALIFIED MORTGAGE PROFESSIONAL

Here are some ideas for where to start your search for a qualified mortgage professional. To begin, seek out personal recommendations and referrals from friends and associates. Be sure to ask them specific questions like:

- Were your calls returned promptly?
- Did your mortgage professional take time to answer your questions?
- Did your mortgage professional foresee any problems, and how did they address and solve those that arose?
- Are you still in contact with your mortgage professional?
- Did your mortgage professional deliver on the rates and terms they promised?

Referrals from real estate professionals can also be helpful. They often have relationships with mortgage professionals to whom they refer clients. So much rides on the financing that a good agent will usually recommend a mortgage professional that's tried and tested.

Once you have a good lead on a mortgage professional, the next step is interviewing them. When you speak to a mortgage professional, make sure you believe they are interested in you as a person. Do they ask questions like:

- How long do you plan to live in the home?
- Are you interested in moving to a larger or smaller home?

- Are you aware of the benefits of paying off your home early or would you like me to walk you through that?

If you have credit problems, it's a good idea to seek out loan officers with experience in helping people correct their credit. Ask if they have ideas for what you should do or can guide you to someone able to help you improve your credit score. You'll know quickly by how they answer your questions if they have experience working with impaired credit.

It's also important that you get the sense that the mortgage professional is capable of getting you a competitive rate at reasonable costs. Are they on top of all the different possible options, and do they make sense to you when they explain the ins and outs of home financing?

"I am a team player, I just play for the other team."

It's important to ask yourself whether it feels like the mortgage professional intends to stay in touch with you after helping with your initial home financing. Are they interested in building a long-term professional relationship or is their focus a quick turnaround and making a quick buck at your expense? If it's the latter, keep looking!

Once you've mapped out the questions you want to ask, done your search, and found your Attentive Amy, you're on track for the next step—forming a solid partnership.

OPTIMIZE YOUR RELATIONSHIP

You've done your due diligence and found a first-rate mortgage professional! Your next stop is making the most of this relationship over both the short and the long term. As a first step, establish a variation of the conditions of satisfaction concept we explored earlier in the book. These will help you clarify with your mortgage professional what both your and their expectations are over the course of the home buying process.

Here are some key conditions that I recommend you propose to your mortgage professional:

- Clear communication throughout the entire process, even when there may be bad news to report.
- Prompt return of calls, same day if possible.
- Willingness to explain the ins and outs of home financing as they relate to your situation, answering all your questions, and making sure you have a clear understanding of all issues.
- Prompt notification when your loan application is submitted, with an estimated timeline for when it will be reviewed and most likely approved by the lender.
- Immediate updates on any development in the mortgage approval process.
- 100% commitment to getting your loan approved and closed on time.
- Working to get you a competitive rate with a loan package that fits your needs and aspirations.
- The desire to work with you and your real estate professional as part of your home buying team.

- Interest in a long-term relationship you can depend on that provides expert advice and service that addresses all your home financing needs.

I believe it's wise that the mortgage professional also articulate clear conditions of satisfaction regarding what they expect from you:

- Promptly return calls, same day if possible.
- Provide them any requested updated financial information within two days, three days max.
- Be understanding if your lender makes requests for information beyond what they originally anticipated.
- Once your loan application is submitted, stay with your lender and don't switch to a competitor midstream. They've done an enormous amount of work on your behalf.
- Once your loan interest rate is locked, don't cancel the deal with the lender in the hope of getting a lower rate from them or another lender. Lenders are penalized if they don't fund loans that are locked.
- Appreciate all the work they're doing on your behalf and refer your friends and associates who are looking for financing for a new or existing home.
- Never move down payment funds into another account without first speaking with your mortgage professional.
- Never close accounts if you are drawing down payment funds from them.
- Never open new credit accounts without first speaking to your mortgage professional.
- Minimize credit card usage as much as possible during the escrow or contract period.
- Don't apply for any credit of any kind.

- Don't interrupt any flow of income. If you are on hourly pay, you may have to come up with a current pay stub. If the amount is lower than what it was when you initially applied, it can impact your loan terms and approval.

Once you've found a mortgage professional you like, I recommend that your first step is walking through these conditions of satisfaction with them. If they're super positive and appreciate your forthrightness regarding expectations, you've almost certainly found a great mortgage professional. If they have a lukewarm or negative reaction or are dismissive of your conditions, look for another mortgage professional pronto!

YOU WANT A LONG-TERM RELATIONSHIP

You may wonder, "Why do I want a long-term relationship with my mortgage professional? Isn't the idea to work with the professional and then, once I have my financing, I'm all set?" That short-term thinking is old-fashioned and doesn't understand the new world of real estate and home financing we live in today. Let me explain.

There are at least four big reasons for building a long-term relationship with your mortgage professional:

- You'll almost certainly explore refinancing your new home, whether to get better rates or to pull out cash in order remodel your home. Your mortgage professional has all your financial information, knows your situation, can quickly explain options, make recommendations, and take actions.
- You may want to buy an investment or rental property. Your mortgage professional can be a tremendous asset in helping you explore options.

- They can be a great *door opener* to other local professionals who can help turn your new home into a key asset and the foundation of your long-term financial security. They know the top CPAs, financial planners, contractors, and insurance agents in your community and can make introductions that get you first-rate attention and service.
- Nurture a healthy relationship with your mortgage professional because they're human and, if your interactions with them are positive, they'll go the extra mile, give you top notch service, and get you excellent results.

Let's now turn to an area that mortgage professionals know a great deal about—pre-qualification and pre-approval letters.

PRE-QUALIFICATION AND PRE-APPROVAL LETTERS

I've found people are often confused about whether they need a pre-qualification letter or a pre-approval letter. These are two very different documents. A pre-qualification letter from a lender is based primarily on verbal, non-verified information that you provide. A pre-approval letter is issued after a lender has verified all of your relevant information and given you a preliminary loan approval.

A pre-approval lets your real estate professional and potential sellers know you're serious and can buy the property they're selling. Virtually no sellers will pull a property off the market for a buyer who isn't already pre-approved. In today's world, where you're competing against buyers who can make all cash offers because they don't need financing, a solid pre-approval letter from a skilled mortgage professional is, in many cases, equal to a cash offer. This is especially true if you aren't trying to sell your current house while trying to buy a new one.

Let's dig deeper now into the process of getting pre-approved for your loan.

YOUR LOAN AND PRE-APPROVAL PROCESS

When we explored the three C's of mortgage financing we covered most of the information required to get rolling on the loan pre-approval process, but let's do a quick review. Here is some of the information that goes on your loan application:

- Gross income—for you and your spouse or partner. This includes your salary, retirement income, interest income, spousal support, child support, etc. The loan application is based solely on the income you are currently generating.
- Credit score and credit report.
- Monthly debt-related expenses, such as minimum monthly payments on items like auto loans and credit cards.
- Total assets available for your down payment and closing costs.

With this information, your mortgage professional and the lender will calculate the all-important debt-to-income ratio that helps determine your capability to pay back a loan.

Your mortgage professional will run your loan application through one of the underwriting engines provided by Fannie Mae or Freddie Mac and receive a credit loan approval. As discussed earlier, this is subject to the appraisal and formal approval by underwriting, which is where any kinks are worked out with your lender.

I cannot emphasize too strongly that after you have been pre-approved for a mortgage, don't open new credit card accounts, take out additional loans for anything, or run up your credit card accounts. Such actions may seriously jeopardize your chance of getting the loan for which you've been pre-approved because any significant change in your credit status can impact the lender's final decision on actually funding the loan.

Here is a cautionary tale about a client named Jennifer who came to me to help secure home financing. We quickly worked through the loan pre-approval process and got her a great rate. Her realtor helped find a lovely house, their bid was accepted, they went into escrow, and everything was looking fantastic.

Right before closing, Jennifer drove up to her appointment with me in a brand new car. While she was super excited about the new car, I could not believe what I was seeing. I had warned her—over and over—not to buy anything new on credit until after the loan is closed. Now I was hoping for the best and fearing the worst because I knew the lender would rerun her credit report at closing.

Her new car purchase overloaded her debt and she no longer qualified for her loan. It looked like Jennifer would be unable to close on her home and would lose her new home AND her deposit. We ultimately pulled together the necessary financing, although at less beneficial terms, and Jennifer got her new home. Because she didn't follow her mortgage professional's explicit instructions, she came within a whisker of losing everything.

Another important factor to always keep in mind is that the lender wants to be 100% sure that no money involved in your transaction has been laundered. This is a big deal to lenders. While your down payment funds aren't likely from selling drugs, the lender will verify the source of money you're using for your down payment, closing costs, and cash reserves.

Any personal funds you intend to use in your down payment must be *seasoned funds* that have been in your bank account for at least sixty days. Make certain that any large deposits to your bank account are made at least sixty days out from when you begin to share your financial information with a potential lender. This time period does not, however, apply to gift funds. You can present those to the lender during the loan process.

Right before they fund your loan, lenders may re-confirm the source of the money you're using for the above items. If there's a change in the accounts where the money came from during the pre-approval process, they can put a hold on funding while they re-verify all of your information—something you don't want to experience again. Remember, the lender will require that you provide the source of any deposits into your accounts, starting with amounts as low as $500 based on your income.

Let me tell you a story of a couple who had money spread out across numerous bank accounts, with many deposits and transfers among the accounts. The husband thought it would help them get an excellent loan if he listed all his bank accounts on his loan application. They immediately ran into problems because every large deposit on their bank statement needed to be verified by the lender, and they had many large deposits.

A second challenge they faced was the lender demanded that they document all transfers between their accounts. The husband was always moving his money from one account to another, searching for better investment deals and making transfers between at least five different accounts. These actions led to an endless process of providing the lender with explanations of the purpose and source of the funds, along with numerous backup documents. This process delayed the couple's ability to get home financing in place and find a new home.

The lessons to be learned are that you should only list on your loan application the minimum number of accounts needed to show assets that qualify you for a loan, and you should have as few transfers as possible between accounts. This will save an enormous amount of time and stress.

Also, when making large deposits into the account where you have your down payment funds, notify your lender in advance and be ready to provide documentation regarding the sources of such funds. I recently had a client who had a large tax refund that he deposited the week before closing and the lender flagged it and required documentation, almost delaying the entire closing process.

"... And how long have you had this irrational fear that you'll never get a mortgage?"

If gift funds are in your list of assets, you must provide the lender with a letter from a family member giving the gift and, in some cases, verify the source of the gift funds. If the family member contributing the funds is hesitant to provide their bank statements, find a lender willing to work with you even if they can't verify the source.

Once you have your loan pre-approval letter in hand, you are ready to engage in the hunt for the perfect property in earnest!

THE CFPB—YOUR NEW BEST FRIEND

A primary question in every home buyer's mind is "How much will it cost me to buy a home after we add up the cost of the mortgage plus all the other related fees and charges?" Recent legislation has mandated that the cost estimates that lenders and service providers give you at the beginning of the application process remain the same, or close to it, when you sign your closing loan documents. The Consumer Financial Protection Bureau, or CFPB, is the federal agency that enforces these laws.

CFPB policies make sure that home buyers are fully informed at the beginning of the loan process regarding the loan terms that lenders offer. They also ensure that buyers have the opportunity to review costs before the closing date and aren't rushed to accept terms they don't agree with or understand. At the heart of these policies are two forms that lenders must give to all borrowers: the *Loan Estimate* and the *Closing Disclosure*. Let's take a quick look at each of them.

The *Loan Estimate* must be given by the lender to all borrowers within three business days after they file a complete loan application. It provides a summary of all loan terms, including the type of loan, interest rate, APR, monthly payments, loan amount, closing costs, title insurance cost, origination fees, appraisal costs, and lock rate information. It also includes the *Total Interest Percentage,* which essentially shows the total amount of interest you pay over the life of the loan.

Prior to the closing, the lender must provide you with the *Closing Disclosure* document three business days before you are allowed to sign loan documents. It includes a detailed accounting of all closing fees and final loan terms. It initiates a mandatory three-day waiting period, during which the home buyer can review all terms and costs without pressure to sign final documents until they fully understand and discuss any concerns with their lender and a real estate professional.

As part of the CFPB's *Know Before You Owe* mortgage initiative, it's mandatory that at the beginning of the loan process lenders provide all home buyers with the *CFPB Home Loan Toolkit* to help them fully understand the *Loan Estimate* and *Closing Disclosure* forms. The toolkit features interactive worksheets, checklists, and research tips to help home buyers seek out and find necessary information. You can download the kit from the CFPB website at the following address: http://files.consumerfinance.gov/f/201503_cfpb_your-home-loan-toolkit-web.pdf.

Generally speaking, the closing process takes thirty to forty-five days, depending on your lender.

Download and read through the CFPB toolkit early in your home buying process. It contains a lot of excellent information, far more than we can review here. The key is to read through the toolkit before applying for a loan, so you have a clear understanding of home buying costs and what to expect from your lender. While the new disclosure process should protect you against worse case scenarios when dealing with unscrupulous or unprofessional lenders, your ultimate protection is working with an expert mortgage professional.

DON'T BE CRAZY—FIND A REAL ESTATE PROFESSIONAL

When buying or selling your home, mortgage financing is so closely linked with real estate services that I can't emphasize too much the value of using a qualified real estate professional.

I've seen the good, the bad, and the ugly of real estate professionals. I've watched the ease with which a true professional handles a purchase from beginning to end. When challenges and problems arise, a professional agent will successfully handle the issues.

CAN WE CALL A *REALTOR* NOW?!

Some home buyers believe they can handle the process themselves. It's tempting to think you can save some cash or buy at a lower price by working directly with the seller. It's my experience, however, that most buyers fail to ask all the important questions, identify danger signs that can later become problems, and often find themselves in lawsuits or property-related legal issues.

If you are a first-time home buyer, beware of a seller not represented by an agent who tells you that working directly with them will save you lots of money. Working directly with a seller can be very frustrating, especially when they keep changing the terms or push you to close without adequately getting the house inspected— something that happened to a client of mine. The flaws in his house showed up later, but the cost of suing the seller was more than the cost of just paying for the repairs themselves.

Whether you're a buyer or seller, hiring a real estate professional is imperative because they know the right and wrong way to make a home sale and have a legal obligation to protect you. Agents are required to carry Errors & Omissions insurance policy. These policies cover you and help underwrite the cost of legal representation if you sue for repayment because the unseen flaws in a property are egregious enough.

Buying a new home can be one of life's most stressful experiences. It involves thousands of dollars and can feel very personal and emotional. The hallmark of real estate and mortgage professionals is that they care about your transaction as much as you do and will do everything in their power to make the process as positive as possible. Their core values are akin to a wonderful saying that I learned from my friend Joanie Young, one of the best real estate professionals in the business: "Service first, sales will follow."

KEYS TO FINDING A TOP-NOTCH REAL ESTATE PROFESSIONAL

The path to finding a good real estate professional is similar to identifying a qualified mortgage professional, so much so that my first recommendation is that when you start your search, go back to our sections on finding a mortgage professional and proposing conditions of satisfaction because the same strategies apply.

One additional suggestion is that you attend some open houses and engage agents there in conversation. In my experience, agents who do open houses keep informed on the neighborhood where they're working, so if it's in an area you're focused on, be sure to talk with them.

You can't have a long conversation at an open house, but you can get a sense of whether the agent is someone you relate to and can provide clear explanations and information. One caveat is that it's generally not advisable to use the agent at an open house as your agent for buying a property if the seller has already retained them. Representing both the buyer and seller is called dual representation and creates a potential conflict of interest for the agent. That said, if you like the agent, I've seen situations where dual representation works out fine for both the buyer and seller.

FIND YOUR NEW HOME—NOW

Stage Two of your home buying process is truly exciting. This is the moment for which you've been preparing! You have your real estate professional and mortgage professional, you're officially pre-approved for a loan, you're ready to find your dream home, make an offer and have it accepted.

With your pre-approval in hand, you and your real estate professional know the price range and types of homes you're qualified to buy. You can now start working as a team to find properties that meet as many of your requirements as possible. You should both be actively engaged in this quest, especially in situations where houses can go on the market and sell within a matter of days—or hours sometimes. When your agent says "jump," you need to be ready to jump and check out homes coming on the market!

Once you find a house within your price range that you like, your real estate professional will put together an offer. You can make an offer that matches the listing price or is below or above it. Making the right offer is where your agent's understanding of the market makes all the difference.

Your mortgage professional is also crucial to a successful offer because they write the pre-approval letter detailed for the home on which you're making an offer. This letter is often the basis for whether the seller chooses your offer over other ones on the table. Not only is a mortgage professional's letter crucial, but their reputation in the real estate and financing community is important. If the seller's agent knows that your mortgage professional has a long history of successfully closing deals, that may tip the scales in your favor. Your mortgage professional may even call the seller's agent to tell them that you're financially sound and your pre-approval letter is exceptionally strong. The last thing that anyone wants—including your agent, the listing agent, and your mortgage professional—is for your financing to blow up in the middle of the process.

Your offer is either accepted, countered—the seller proposes a higher sales price, shorter closing period, or other conditions—or rejected for another offer. Sometimes your offer is accepted as a backup in case the first accepted offer falls through.

When your offer is accepted, get ready for an exciting ride, because the closing process kicks in and a whole lot has to happen over a very short time.

CHAPTER 11

YOUR OFFER IS ACCEPTED. NOW WHAT?

Congratulations! The seller has accepted your offer to purchase your new home. This is one of the most exciting moments of your life, but there's still work you need to do. You're now entering Phase Three of the home buying process.

Depending on the state where you're buying your new home, you're entering the *escrow* or the *contract process*. We'll refer to it as the *closing* process. This process can be an obstacle course where the capabilities of your real estate professional and mortgage professional make all the difference, providing you with a smooth ride or turning your life into hell on earth.

The closing process protects the rights of all parties involved and facilitates a course of action that leads as quickly as possible to closing the deal and getting you into your new home. It begins when the seller accepts your offer and ends when your lender funds your loan. The deed is recorded with the county, and all monies are released. This process enables all key parties to be paid, including the seller, so that you can take possession of your new home.

There are numerous variables in the closing process. To make all the elements easier to grasp, I've divided Phase Three into the two stages in the infographic below.

KEY CLOSING PHASES

Stage One of Closing	Stage Two of Closing
Home enters escrow when your offer is accepted	Review Closing Disclosure from lender
Loan submitted for formal approval	Wait three days to sign loan documents
Loan Estimate is emailed or mailed	Sign loan documents
Home is inspected	Lender is notified and/or loan documents are returned to them
Identify and negotiate any repairs with seller	Final review by lender before and/or after loan documents are signed:
Release inspection contingency	+ Lender pulls soft credit to verify no new credit
Home is appraised	+ Match down-payment funds with funds disclosed on original app.
Lock the interest rate	+ Lender verbally verifies employment
Appraisal is completed	Your loan is funded
Receive formal loan approval	Your loan is recorded
Satisfy remaining lender's loan conditions	Congratulations! You get the keys to your new home!
Release contingencies for loan approval and appraisal	
Loan receives a "clear to close"	

GETTING THE CLOSING PROCESS ROLLING

Once your offer is accepted, you and the seller agree to a purchase contract. This document includes the amount you will pay for the property and the amount you'll deposit to hold the property. This is called an "earnest money deposit," and is generally 3% of the purchase price. In some cases, you can negotiate a lower amount.

You and the seller must now agree to retain an escrow officer or real estate attorney who we refer to as the closing officer. The listing agent usually recommends the closing officer, who manages the closing process, tracks all the conditions to be met by you and the seller, holds funds deposited by you, processes the paperwork, and disburses funds from your lender to the appropriate parties.

The closing process ground rules are agreed to by all parties up front. Key items include the length of the contract period, which is the date you plan to close on the property, the amount of your deposit, the schedule for when you sign off on the appraisal and loan contingencies, and the date you must deliver funds to complete your purchase.

CONTINGENCIES AND INSPECTIONS

The closing process includes a series of inspections to be performed and contingencies on which the buyer must sign off. This process protects both you and the seller. At the beginning of the closing process, the buyer signs off on a detailed schedule for contingencies. Not signing off according to the schedule can jeopardize the entire deal, so it's important that you, as the buyer, understand everything to which you agree.

Here are the main contingencies:

- Property Inspection: You must release this contingency, usually within five to seven days from the date that your offer is accepted. You pay for the inspection and choose the inspector. A good real estate professional will give you the names of two to three potential inspectors and let you make the call. Key areas inspected include plumbing, heating, gas, electric, window and door functionality, any water damage, chimney issues, mold, or other conditions. The inspector sends you a report with recommendations for repairs where needed. The lender does not see the inspection report. If repairs are required, you may informally ask the inspector to tell you the potential cost of needed repairs. The seller is responsible for the repairs but can choose to sell as is. In some cases, the seller might refuse to do the repairs but drop the purchase price by the repair amount, or pay for your closing costs, or suggest that other arrangements be negotiated. If you have a concern about the report, this is a good time to talk to your real estate professional about negotiating with the seller for a solution you're comfortable with. If the seller resists, consider canceling the deal and having your deposit returned.

- Termite and radon inspection, based on the state where you live. These inspections may not be required as part of the sales contract, and the seller and the buyer must both agree to them.

- The *appraisal contingency* must be released by the buyer, usually within seventeen to twenty-one days from the date the offer is accepted—based on the state where you live. An appraiser determines the value of the house. The appraisal is sent to the lender who reviews it. If they agree with the appraised value, the process moves forward. If they have concerns, they ask their in-house appraiser to do a *desk review* or to visit the property and conduct their own appraisal. Until the lender agrees with the value provided in the original appraisal or provides a new value, do not release the appraisal contingency. If the appraiser sees deficiencies with the property, they'll note them in their report. For instance, if they observe that the roof is damaged, they'll recommend a roof certification. If that happens, the lender asks for a roof certification from a roofing contractor. They also want the appraiser to look closely at conformance with health and safety guidelines, such as double strapping a water heater or protecting gas lines. Where deficiencies occur in this area, the property must be re-inspected after the seller addresses the issue, which can delay the process. Carefully review the appraiser's report in its entirety before releasing this contingency. If you have any concerns, consult with your mortgage or real estate professional.

- Depending on the state where the transaction is taking place, the loan contingency must be released by you within seventeen to twenty-one days, unless otherwise negotiated. You release the contingency when you have assurance from your mortgage professional that the loan is fully approved, that you're your cleared to close, and you can order loan documents. After your loan is approved, the lender may ask for additional items to finalize the approval. NEVER release the loan contingency until you and your mortgage professional are 100% confident your loan will fund. Once you release the loan contingency, your initial deposit is no longer refundable.

When you've released all the above contingencies, the seller can breathe a sigh of relief and know the deal will almost certainly be done! At this point, the buyer starts lining up their moving truck and professional services like cleaners and painters to prepare the home for move in once your home closes. Maintain flexibility regarding dates for repair work to commence until you know with certainty the date your loan documents will be ready to sign and you can close on your home.

LOCKING YOUR INTEREST RATE

When it comes to the closing process, understanding what it means to lock your interest rate should be high on the list. Locking a rate can determine your actual interest rate and the amount of money you pay over the life of your loan. It's such a big deal that it's an essential part of federal legislation regarding disclosures from lenders.

Even with all the government intervention on this issue, people run into serious problems. For example, imagine you are ready to close on a home that has been under contract for forty-five days. At the last minute, the lender tells you the interest rate quote they made was too low, or they failed to lock your rate, or the lock expired, and your rate is rising by 1%. Do you cancel escrow and tell the lender to cancel the loan?

This is a complicated decision, especially when other buyers and sellers may be depending on you to close on their home because you already released your contingencies. Most buyers feel pressure to accept the higher rate because they want the process over with. They may also be at risk of violating the terms of their contract if they fail to close on time.

Any lender can give you the song and dance of how low their interest rates are. Delivering on the interest rate that led you to their door is an entirely different matter. That's why it's essential to lock in a rate before you get too far in the closing process.

WHAT DOES "LOCKING IN A RATE" MEAN?

Locking an interest rate means the lender commits to giving you a specific rate at an agreed to cost for a set time period. For example, let's say you just signed a purchase agreement for a new home that closes in thirty days and a lender quoted you an interest rate of 4.375%. You will want to lock it for thirty days, so if your home purchase closes within that time, you're guaranteed a 4.375% interest rate. You should also find out if the lender is confident that they can close within thirty days or the proposed escrow period.

If you don't lock your rate and let it float, you may face a higher rate when you decide to lock it later on. An important consideration regarding whether to lock your rate is that if you play the market and interest rates increase, you may no longer qualify to buy the home.

A mortgage professional can help you through the process of locking your rate. First, you decide the interest rate you want and determine the corresponding charge or points a particular rate will cost. The lock period is primarily determined by the closing date you've agreed to with the seller. Most lenders offer up to sixty-day locks. The longer the lock period, the more it costs you because the lender must pay additional fees to guarantee your interest rate over the longer time frame.

When a lender agrees to lock your interest rate, it's called a *forward commitment* or a *hedge*. A forward commitment is essentially an insurance policy to protect lenders if rates increase while you are in the closing process.

If interest rates decrease during the initial lock period, it's not likely you get the lower rate. A few lenders offer a *float down policy* if interest rates fall. Rates must decrease dramatically before lenders will give you the lower rate.

If interest rates decline after you lock your loan and your lender does not have a float down option, it's not advisable to push them for the lower rate. First, canceling a locked loan can have serious consequences for the lender. All lenders have what is called *pull through*. This is the percentage of locked loans that get funded. If lenders have a high cancellation rate of locked loans, they get cut off from their funding sources or have to raise their interest rates because their borrowing costs will increase.

Be aware that your lender has no control over the interest rates. Consider the following analogy. If I buy a stock for $10 and its value drops to $5, I can't go back to the stockbroker and ask him to buy it back for $10. Or if I buy a stock for $10 and its value goes up to $15, the broker can't come to me and ask for another $5. So when you lock a rate, you are buying that rate regardless of how overall interest rates may fluctuate.

When deciding how long to lock your rate, remember that while your lender may offer you the lowest rate on the planet, if they can't get your loan funded by the time your lock expires, you never had the exceptional rate they promised to begin with.

WHAT IF YOUR LOCK EXPIRES BEFORE YOUR LOAN IS FUNDED?

If your lock is expiring before your loan is funded, one of four things will happen:

- Interest rates increase, you lose the locked rate and have to take the higher rate. This may cause problems qualifying for a loan.
- Interest rates drop or are at the original rate you locked. In most cases, you get the original rate you locked because lenders don't want to incentivize borrowers to let their lock expire just to get a lower rate. Also, be aware there may be a fee for relocking.
- Rates really plummet. The lender may, in rare cases, consider renegotiating so you can receive the lower rate.
- The lender lets you extend your lock period before your current lock expires. There are usually additional fees associated with this, so discuss this with your mortgage professional.

Before locking your rate, find out whether your lender will extend the lock for an additional period. This option is very helpful, especially when rates are increasing. And remember, the longer the extension, the higher the fee.

Not all lenders will extend your locked rate. Some will do something called *worst case pricing* and relock the loan at a higher rate. This is why it's imperative to have a mortgage professional walk you through this process. The key is getting it right with the initial lock and trusting the integrity of your lender.

TO LOCK OR NOT TO LOCK

When you're in this business for a while, you discover that interest rates go up much faster than they come down. When rates start to rise they can jump a quarter point—say from 4.5% interest to 4.75—in the blink of an eye, but then take weeks or months to drop a quarter of a point. I recommend locking a rate near the beginning of the closing process, so you don't need to worry about rates rising or not qualifying because they jumped.

If you decide not to lock, ask your lender to keep an eye on the rates for you. No lender can predict the direction future rates will go, but with the right knowledge and tools they can tell you the general direction interest rates are moving and when is a smart time to lock your rate. Mortgage professionals subscribe to services that offer a wealth of information on the disposition of rates on a daily basis. I certainly do, and it allows me to have intelligent conversations with my clients about locking at the optimal point.

DOWN THE HOMESTRETCH

You are now so close to your goal of owning your own home that the excitement and anticipation are building. The appraisal has been completed and sent to you and the lender. Assuming the appraised value came in at or above the purchase price and any repairs have been carried out by the seller, you have removed the appraisal contingency and moved forward with final loan approval.

You also already received the property inspection report and termite report. Again, assuming everything was in good order, or you have worked out repair arrangements with the seller to everyone's satisfaction, you've released the inspection contingencies. You have also released the loan contingency.

Once you've released all of these contingencies, the next step is having your mortgage professional ask the lender to draw up the loan documents. The lender may request any final additional documentation that has been requested by underwriting, and you and your mortgage professional will want to move quickly to address any of their concerns.

I've said this before, but please, during the entire closing process, don't buy anything on credit. When the lender does the final review of recent credit inquiries and outstanding debt on your credit report, if your debt has increased they can use that as grounds to increase your interest rate or reevaluate whether to give you a loan at all!

HEADING FOR THE FINISH LINE

You're in the final stage of closing, the final step in buying your home! You've released all the contingencies. You've provided the lender with all the final documentation they requested. Your interest rate is locked, and you've signed off on the Closing Disclosure. The final loan documents are being drawn by the lender and will be sent to the closing agent. You are scheduled to sign the final loan documents.

Key participants in the loan signing meeting include the buyer, the notary, and, possibly, the closing officer. The seller may participate, depending on the state where the transaction is taking place. I recommend that your mortgage professional is with you to answer any questions you have about anything regarding the closing disclosure. At the very least, ask your mortgage professional to be available by phone for questions. Do not sign off on the loan documents until you get answers to your questions.

Once the loan documents are signed, your lender is notified or the documents are returned to the lender. If they have not done so previously, the lender will do one final internal check of your credit and verify there are no new debts. They also confirm that your down payment deposit is from the account submitted with the loan application, you're still employed, and everything from the beginning of the process is unchanged. Please remember, if you have any new debts, they are counted against your debt-to-income ratio and may result in your no longer qualifying for the mortgage. If you have no new debts, you should be in great shape.

PICK UP THE KEYS ALREADY

Just two key steps remain. First, your down payment and closing funds are transferred to the title company via a wire or cashiers check. Then the lender must fund the loan by sending a wire with the agreed amount to the title company or the closing attorney. If you send your down payment via a wire, it's transferred through the Federal Reserve. In rare instances, the Federal Reserve may place a hold on the wire for further inspection. When wiring your down payment, give yourself a little buffer by sending it at least one or two days before the closing date. Keep in mind that wiring the funds is preferred because holds can be placed on a cashier's check.

Upon receipt of the wire from the lender, the closing officer immediately jumps into action. They request that the county record the deed or mortgage they've sent, notify the title company, and disperse funds to all the appropriate parties, including the seller, the seller's listing agent, and your real estate professional.

Congratulations! You are officially the proud owner of your own home. The first stage in your homeownership journey is complete, and an exciting next phase is about to begin.

What are your waiting for? Pick up the keys and call the movers!!!

PART 5

YOUR PATH TO FINANCIAL SECURITY

CHAPTER 12

MAKE YOUR MORTGAGE WORK FOR YOU, NOT AGAINST YOU

A big step in turning your home into a source of financial security is correctly managing your mortgage. There are three keys to guaranteeing that your mortgage works FOR YOU and not AGAINST YOU. All three focus on building up as much equity in your home as quickly as possible and increasing your equity until you pay off your mortgage and own your home outright. We covered some of these strategies before, but they're so important we should review them now that you are in possession of your new home!

Your home equity is the positive difference between the fair market value of your home and the outstanding balance of all the loans or debt you've secured against your home. If the value of your home is $400,000 and you have an outstanding mortgage against it totaling $300,000, you have $100,000 in equity. Your equity increases when you pay down the principal on your mortgage, when you make improvements to your property that increase its value, or when your property value rises because of external market dynamics. Let's focus on the two levers that you control and where your actions can make a big difference.

Your first lever is managing your mortgage and making it work for you. Here are the three ways to do that.

First, pay down the principal as soon and as fast as possible. We discussed this in the section on amortization.

Second, if you refinance to get better terms, structure the refinancing so you can pay your mortgage off more quickly rather than just reducing your monthly mortgage payments. The key is not to pay less each month, but to pay off the mortgage and increase your equity as quickly as possible. That's how you can build wealth and financial security.

Third, don't take out additional loans or lines of credit against your home unless you use the funds to increase your home's value over time.

A quick word on increasing the value of your home through regular ongoing maintenance and home improvement or renovation projects. When I talk about treating your home as a sacred trust, caring for it is part of the deal. Your home could well be the single most valuable asset you own. If you respect it, care for it, maintain it, and upgrade it wisely, you're treating it as a sacred trust, and it will reward you and your family financially, emotionally, and spiritually.

If you are a couple who shares the ownership of your home, I strongly encourage you to jointly make all financial and maintenance decisions regarding your home and your mortgage. This will strengthen your relationship, give you a common sense of purpose, and enable you to celebrate your increased financial wealth and stability together. It will also reduce the tension that arises if there are disagreements about priorities and what you, as a couple, value most highly.

TAKING OUT A LINE OF CREDIT—THINK TWICE, AND THEN AGAIN

It has become a common strategy—often promoted by lenders—to encourage homeowners to take out a line of credit on their home in case of an emergency, or to buy a car, invest in a business, or a million other reasons. Let's take a closer look at the risks of this strategy.

First, what is a line of credit? Here is how it works. You've built up $100,000 in equity in your home through the strategies we've discussed. Your lender says, "Hey, let's make your equity work for you. We'll set up a line of credit for $40,000 secured against your home, and you can use that $40,000 for whatever you want. You just pay interest, and you don't even have to pay down any of the principal you've borrowed. You can pay it down if you want, but we won't make you do it." That seems like a pretty sweet deal. Wrong!

What's wrong with this story? First, in most cases you'll be required to start paying down the principal on the line of credit after ten years and the lender will convert it to a fully amortized loan with a higher fixed rate than you are paying now. Let's take that $40,000 line of credit. A 6% interest-only payment is $200 a month. It's tempting to think this is cheap money, however, a line of credit is subject to rate increases and in ten years your new payment could be $400. By the time you pay off your $40,000 line of credit, it could cost you approximately $50,000 in interest, for a total of $90,000. A line of credit is not cheap money—not by any stretch of the imagination.

Second, if you're borrowing money to cover your ongoing cash flow, you're living above your means. If you use your line of credit to buy food, once you eat the food all that's left is more debt. The better solution is to reduce your expenses or increase your income. Borrowing money increases your costs because you're now paying interest. So never take out a line of credit to cover ongoing expenses.

Third, as previously discussed, beware of borrowing on your home to fund your business. You're potentially undermining the financial security you've achieved and investing your equity in a speculative venture with no guaranteed return, and the possibility you might lose it all. There are lots of other places to find capital for your business, and if those don't pan out, it might be your business plan is too risky, and it's time to rethink it.

Fourth, if you're buying a car, get a car loan. Don't buy it by pulling equity out of your home. When you're incurring debt, distribute the risk across various debt vehicles so that if you run into trouble, you'll only lose your car and not your home as well.

Lenders created personal lines of credit as short-term debt vehicles with interest rates tied to the prime rate. If you don't repay the debt quickly, you're subject to the volatility in the market and, if the prime rate starts rising, your interest payments rise as well. This eventual rise in your payments is why lenders are happy to let you pay interest only. You're not reducing your debt, and you're paying them more and more in interest. That's a sweet deal for them, but not for you.

Your lender will eventually demand that you start paying down the principal on the line of credit and your payments could skyrocket to two or three times the amount you've come to expect.

Here is my checklist for deciding to get a line of credit:

- Is what you're buying or investing in an asset that will appreciate over time?
- Have you explored all the other possible ways to get the funds without securing more debt against your home?
- Will you be able to pay off the line of credit as a short-term debt within an 18-month period?
- If you can't pay back the money you borrow within 18 months, what's your plan to pay it back and how quickly can you do it?

When thinking about getting a line of credit on your house, think twice, or maybe three or four times, and run through my checklist before you pull the trigger.

REFINANCING CAN BE A GOOD THING

You can't turn on the radio these days without hearing a lender pitch to refinance your home mortgage. It may be the case that what they pitch is too good to be true, but I recommend that you keep track of your refinancing options and make a move at the optimal moment.

Everyone's situation is different, but here are some basic guidelines when considering refinancing. You should seriously consider refinancing if:

- Mortgage interest rates have dropped since you first got your mortgage. The rule of thumb once was that if the refinance rate you can get is 2% or more below your existing rate, refinancing is a good move. However, with all the *no fee, no costs* refinancing options now available, refinancing can be worthwhile even if the new rate is just ½ percent lower than your existing one. That said, there are two key points you should know. First and foremost, when refinancing, do everything possible to continue making the same size payments you're making now, which means there's a good possibility you can pay off your loan much faster. Second, consider how long you've been making payments on your mortgage. For example, if you have been making payments on your mortgage for fifteen years it may not make sense to start over again with a 30-year fixed mortgage unless you specifically want to lower your mortgage payment. If you do refinance based on lower rates and the like, think about the option of refinancing based on the term of loan you have left. If you have fifteen years left to pay on the loan, then get a 10- or 15-year fixed rate loan. A good mortgage professional can provide you with an analysis of whether it's worth it to refinance.

- You can lower your interest rate, pay no fees, AND get a better type of loan, for instance, going from a variable to a fixed interest rate or from a 30-year to a 15-year term.
- You can combine your first and second loans or line of credit and reduce your interest payments in the process.

Refinancing is essentially the restructuring of your debt. If the restructuring leads to a better type of loan with lower interest rates or a shorter term, consider refinancing your home. One note of caution is that refinancing your original purchase money loan may change the designation of the loan from a non-recourse to a recourse loan. This is state specific and is something to speak with your attorney or mortgage advisor about.

CHAPTER 13

KEEP IN TOUCH

I'm so excited for you as you set off on your journey to buying and owning a home. It's my sincere hope that the knowledge and tools you have gained during our journey together will empower you to wisely choose and carefully manage your relationships with the mortgage professional and the real estate professional who are the key players on your personal home buying team.

I've been fortunate to witness, many times over, how buying and owning a home, when done with care, can be the experience of a lifetime. May the lessons I've shared enable you to find the joy, happiness, and financial security that's possible through owning a home, and help you to avoid the pitfalls and heartbreak others have experienced because they didn't have the knowledge or guidance required to navigate buying and owning their home.

My passion is to do whatever I can to support you throughout your home buying and ownership process. I love hearing from readers, whether you have specific questions that we haven't answered or if you have a wonderful story about how this book helped you achieve your homeownership goals.

Please visit my website at www.mainstreetloans.com for the latest information regarding securing financing. Don't hesitate to send me an email at JohnMallett@MainStreetLoans.com if you have any thoughts, questions or stories you want to share.

I look forward to hearing from you and wish you the greatest success in finding, buying, and owning the home of your dreams!

APPENDIX

This appendix includes two sections that address important issues people often ask me about that you may find of interest. The first focuses on the risks of using your home equity as a source of funds for *playing the market*. The second one looks at *bad debt* and its negative impact on people when they use debt to fund a lifestyle that is beyond their means and unsustainable.

DON'T RISK YOUR HOME WHEN PLAYING THE MARKET

Before the mortgage meltdown, home values were skyrocketing, and the stock market was experiencing consistent gains. I regularly received calls from clients considering whether they should take money out of their home through refinancing or a line of credit to invest in the stock market or other ventures. As a new home buyer with limited equity in your home, this may not be an immediate issue. But when property values are rising there are scores of financial advisors who believe that investing money in the market is a far better idea than paying off your mortgage early or even paying it off at all. Their position is that pulling cash out of your home for investment purposes, sometimes called equity stripping, can yield a greater return. Clients often ask my opinion on this strategy, so let's take a closer look at the potential benefits and risks.

If the term, *equity*, is new to you, here is a quick explanation. If you own a home that's valued at $400,000 and owe $250,000 in the form of a loan or mortgage, you have $150,000 in equity. A lender will often make available to you some portion of that $150,000 in the form of a line of credit or a loan, and use your home as collateral. This is cash you can then invest in the stock market or use for other purposes of your own choosing.

Many financial analysts believe it's smarter to invest in the market than maintain equity in your home. If you can get a higher return in the market than the cost of the money you are borrowing on your home, their approach is tempting, and may even be worthwhile. That said, I encourage you to keep the following in mind:

- Investments that bring healthy returns usually carry a higher level of risk. Such risk is especially dangerous for people near retirement or already retired.

- You must continually monitor any investments, and fluctuations in their value can be very stressful, especially when your home is on the line. Is that a stress you want in your life?
- You can lose your entire investment, resulting in higher interest payments on your home-related debt. If you can't cover those payments, you may lose your house.
- Some money coming from return on investment will be taxed, so include that in your return on investment equation.
- No one can give you a 100% iron-clad guarantee that the money you invest in the market is not subject to some level of risk. Some investment products such as U.S. government securities come close to zero risk. If you take no risk at all, it's next to impossible to see your investment in the market grow.

Most of us don't have the expertise to invest money into the market, and not all financial planners and advisors are created equal. I know some who are incredibly talented and help their clients see substantial returns. Others I've met should not even be in the business.

I don't know your financial planner or your personal ability to spot investment opportunities. What I do know is neither you nor your financial planner requires any unique expertise to understand how to pay off your home. Every homeowner can do this regardless of education level or understanding of the market. I've seen many people who regretted taking money out of their home to invest in the market, but very few who were not thrilled to pay off their mortgage and own their home.

Building a financial portfolio that includes a range of types of investments is an essential part of prudent financial planning. If you have a qualified financial planner, there can be significant benefits to investing. In some instances, it may make sense to increase your investment activity rather than to accelerate the paying down of the principal on your home mortgage. That said, I implore you to tread carefully when pulling equity out of your home—and putting your home at risk—so you can invest in the market.

Too often I've watched people pull money out of their home to invest in the stock market and other vehicles, only to see a negative return on investment that results in carrying greater debt and even losing their home. My bottom line is that if you decide to invest in the stock market or other vehicles, don't put the home you own and live in on the line as part of your investment strategy.

BEWARE THE DANGERS OF BAD DEBT

Understanding the dangers of bad debt is important in itself, but is especially important when thinking about buying a home. Carrying even a minimal amount of bad debt can severely impact your ability to get any home financing, let alone your ability to get top-notch loan terms.

We all know it takes no effort at all to acquire debt, especially credit card debt, but that it can take an enormous effort to pay it off. I counsel clients who have debt that is hindering them from reaching their dreams and threatening their health and relationships. What's particularly insidious is how debt sneaks up and then suddenly overwhelms people.

There is good debt and bad debt. Good debt is connected to assets that will likely grow in value over time, like a mortgage on a home. Bad debt is tied to possessions that lose value, often quickly, or support a lifestyle a person can't afford. If I knew in my twenties what I know now, I would have managed my money and looked at debt very differently.

Before exploring the nuts and bolts of debt, here are some overarching principles that I encourage you to follow:

- Have a big picture vision of what you want to do with your life. Ask if the debt you're about to take on will move your life in the direction you want to go or if it is a quick fix to meet a desire that risks draining your resources and sidetracking you from your vision.

- Honor and celebrate the value of living within your means rather than buying things or creating a lifestyle you can only support through debt. It takes discipline to live within your means while working toward long-term goals, but your efforts will be rewarded.

- Have respect for how hard you work for the money you earn. Don't squander your earnings by acquiring debt that means you're working more to pay your lenders than to support a life that you and your family can enjoy.

Follow these principles, and you're on your way to avoiding the heartbreak of living under the crushing burden of debt.

Let's dig deeper into how debt works. To owe a financial debt means you've borrowed money and must pay it back. Whoever lent you the money wants to be paid something extra in the form of fees and interest. So you're obligated to pay back what you borrowed AND a little or a lot more also.

Some people unexpectedly find themselves in deep debt because of a life crisis like an illness that results in huge medical bills. However, the majority of people get into debt trouble for two primary reasons: 1) lack of knowledge; and 2) lack of discipline when managing the money they have or borrowing the money they think they need.

For instance, wouldn't you think twice if you understood that buying a home entertainment center on your credit card for $2,000 and just making recommended minimum monthly payments means carrying that debt for almost 15 years at a rate of 18%, which costs you $1,833 in interest? I regularly counsel people who had no idea the trouble they got into charging for all kinds of purchases and how that was placing a long-term burden on their lives. That's an experience I don't want you to have, so let's look at how to manage the money you have prudently. The most important place to start, especially when trying to get home financing, is understanding your spendable income.

WHAT IS YOUR SPENDABLE INCOME?

A big key to managing money is understanding how much you have available to spend. Whenever I ask clients for their income, they give me their gross income. How many people do you think can tell me their net income after taxes? Almost zero! If you don't know your spendable income, you will come up short at the end of the month and then have to borrow money to make ends meet.

Because you're considering buying a home, you should know your spendable income because it's a big factor in determining the financing available to you.

Your spendable income is not your total salary, but the amount of your paycheck *after* taxes. Let's look at a client named Jim. His income level puts him in the 20% tax bracket. For every dollar he makes, 20 cents goes to federal and state taxes. The math looks like this: $1.00 X 20% = $.20. Jim has $.80 cents remaining out of every dollar after taxes. If his gross salary is $5,000 a month, he pays $1,000 in taxes and his spendable income is $4,000.

Let's say Jim has created a $4,500 a month lifestyle. That's $500 a month more than he can afford. That money must come from somewhere. In Jim's case, he's putting $500 a month on his credit card. After eight months, he's $4,000 in debt.

If the interest rate on the credit card is 18%, the cost of having the $4,000 balance on his credit card is $60 per month. The credit card company wants a repayment on the principal of $10 per month, so his total monthly payment is $70.

Jim's $4,500 a month lifestyle is now even less affordable. His net income remains at $4,000 a month, but, with the monthly $70 payment to the credit card company, he just has $3,930 available for living expenses. With the credit card debt he's paying, he must make

127% more than his basic living expenses just to break even. If Jim only makes the $70 minimum payment on his credit card, it will take him 17 years to pay off the $4,000 that he borrowed in just eight months! When he sees those numbers, he decides to start paying more than the minimum.

Jim now plans to pay off the $4,000 in one year, which means $393 a month goes to the credit card company. Now his spendable income is $3,607, almost $900 below his $4,500 spending rate. Cutting living expenses by 20% or $900 a month can be difficult, so Jim may be hard pressed to make his $393 monthly payment. That's why many people just make the minimum monthly payment and spend years paying off the debt they originally accumulated in a matter of months.

I implore you not to fall into the debt trap like Jim. Think before you get a loan or rack up credit card charges that you can't pay back quickly. Debt adds up a whole lot faster than it can be paid off. One way to look at this that can be sobering is to add up the total number of days, months, or even years you may have to work to earn money that goes to paying interest to your credit card companies and lenders. You may be shocked at the total!

If you already have a lot of debt, the good news is there are strategies for effectively paying it down. I've had many clients who've turned around their debt situation, so don't despair.

Knowing your spendable income is an important first step to living within your means and avoiding debt. The next big step is creating a monthly budget so you can carefully decide how to allocate and spend the funds you have available.

Made in USA - Kendallville, IN
77014_9780998560809
12.05.2022 1323